Our Game:

The Character and Culture of

Lacrosse

by

John M. Yeager

DUDE PUBLISHING
A Division of
National Professional Resources, Inc.
Port Chester, New York

Publisher's Cataloging-in-Publication
(Provided by Quality Books, Inc.)

Yeager, John M.
  Our game : the character and culture of Lacrosse / by
John M. Yeager.
  p. cm.
  Includes bibliographical references and index.
  ISBN 1-887943-99-4

  1. Lacrosse--North America--History. 2. Lacrosse--
Coaching--Moral and ethical aspects. 3. Lacrosse for
children--Psychological aspects. 4. Character.
5. Sportsmanship--Study and teaching.   I. Title.

GV989.Y43 2005   796.34'7
                      QBI05-600214

Cover design by Claudia Menanteau, US Lacrosse

Book design and production by Andrea Cerone,
National Professional Resources, Inc., Port Chester, NY 10573

Dude Publishing
A division of National Professional Resources, Inc.
25 South Regent Street
Port Chester, NY 10573
Toll free: (800) 453-7461
Phone: (914) 937-8879

Visit our web site: www.NPRinc.com

Printed in the United States of America

ISBN 1-887943-99-4

To Gordon Webb -
Whose passion for the game has
made all the difference for me.

Acknowledgments

I am very grateful to those who assisted me in the process of writing this book. John Pirani, head boy's lacrosse coach at Winchester, Mass., High School has been instrumental in grounding me when searching for "what matters most" in this wonderful game. Gordon Webb and Mel McKee, although they many not realize it, instilled a great passion for lacrosse in me.

This book couldn't have been written without the support of US Lacrosse. I thank Steve Stenersen, executive director, Jen Allen, former director of sport development, Beth Reisinger, Josh Christian, Glenn Schorr, Erin Smith, Kath Fenzel, Joe Gold, Jody Martin and Ann Kitt Carpenetti. I thank US Lacrosse's Brian Logue, Paul Krome, and Matt DaSilva for content editing. Erin Millon, former college and US Team standout and former US Lacrosse Women's Director, was instrumental in providing the important history and decisions behind the growth of the women's game. Also, I owe the members of US Lacrosse's Campaign for Excellence committee a great depth of gratitude, especially Dave Antol and John Ourisman, also a member of the US Lacrosse Foundation. The Positive Coaching Alliance's credo resonates throughout the book. Thanks to Kathy Toon and Jan Merryweather for their insights on creating a positive lacrosse culture. Dave, John, and Kathy were also prime movers in the development of the US Lacrosse Standards of Excellence at the Campaign for Excellence Summit in March, 2005. I am grateful for the other members at the summit: Monica Yeakel, Casey Powell, Jenny Riittano, Katie Bedwell, Joanna Lignelli, Adam Werder, Tom Fitzsimmons, Kevin Graham, Chip Rogers, Jay Williams, Erin Brown Millon, Sue Diffenderffer, John Stevenson, Don Stoppenbach, Kim Lenta, Lisa Christiansen and Holly Buckingham.

The following high school coaches provided great insight: Dee Stephan, Jessica Battle, Wendy Kridel, Kristen Corrigan, Dee Stephan, Paul Sieben, Al Rotatori, Alan McCoy, John Piper, Larry Briggs, Gene Zanella, Jim Wilson, Jordy Almgren, Nick Antol, Steve Bristol, Mike Caravana, Shaun Stanton, Steve Connolly, Will Graham, and Bob Shriver.

I appreciate the thoughts of the youth coaches and administrators who are guiding the future of the game: Bob Stevenson, Casey Jackson, Kate Dresher, John Sardella, Tom Zacoi, Jack Light, Jay Williams, Lou Corsetti and Noel Ebner.

A variety of current and former college coaches unselfishly shared their insights on the future of the game: Bowen Holden, Chris Paradis, Missy Foote, Sue Stahl, Ricky Fried, Dom Starsia, Bill Tierney, Dave Pietramala, Tony Seaman, Sid Jamieson, Roy Simmons, Jr., Dave Urick, Greg Cannella, Marc Van Arsdale, Rob Pfeiffer, Jeff Long, Brad Jorgenson, Brad Nasato, Sean Quirk, Dave Campbell, Erin Quinn, Mike Murphy, Kevin Hicks, Keith Bugbee, Mike Murphy, Paul Schimoler, Peter Lasagna, Rob Quinn, Jeff Long, Steve Koudelka, Terry Mangan, Walt Alessi and Paul Wehrum.

I am grateful to Jim Tighe, John Hill, Susie Ganzenmuller, Pat Dillon, Sue Diffenderffer and Matt Palumb for addressing the officials perspective of the game.

I learned much from John Gagliardi and Casey Powell, who as elite players, also share their vast knowledge and passion for the game with youth players.

Adam Werner, Jack Piatelli, and Jenny Riitano, from the Lacrosse industry and Flip Naumberg, co-director of the Vail Tournament gave timely insights into the marketing of the game.

Edwin Delattre, Steve Tigner, Len Zaichkowsky, Jerry Larson, and Adam Naylor who have strong connections at Boston University, have all been instrumental in my philosophical and psychological underpinnings of sport. Their thoughts are embedded in the book. I thank my co-authors of *Character and Coaching,* John Buxton, Amy Baltzell and Wally Bzdell for providing a base to start from with this book. I appreciate the thoughts of John Buxton, Kathy Lintner, the late O'Neill Turner and his son O'Neill of The Culver Academies for their perspective on the cultural and mythological underpinnings to the game. Kudos to Emily (Buxton) McCann, who eloquently shared how lacrosse has influenced her life.

Several members of the US Lacrosse Foundation have provided great motivation for me: Mike Wilcox, the Annual Giving/ Major Gifts Committee Co-Chair and Todd Parchman have given tirelessly to making the game better. I will always be indebted to them for their efforts on the Foundation as well as their support for Culver lacrosse as parents of current and former players.

I thank Martin Seligman and James Pawelski from the Positive Psychology Center at the University of Pennsylvania for reinforcing within me the importance of achieving a sense of pleasure, engagement and meaning in all the things we do.

Most of all, a great deal of admiration is given to my wife, Laura, and daughter, Megan, for their tireless support of my involvement with lacrosse.

John M. Yeager
Culver, Indiana
September, 2005

Publisher's Note

Dude Publishing, a division of National Professional Resources, Inc., is proud to publish this work. We entered into this collaboration with US Lacrosse based upon our prior relationship with John Yeager, and our deep admiration for his passion and commitment to young people's character. We are impressed with the manner in which John has captured the roots of Lacrosse, melded them with today's game, while keeping a vigilant focus on character development, as both a responsibility and opportunity of all stakeholders.

Contents

Foreword I
Introduction V

Section 1 — The Traditions and Culture of the Sport
    Chapter 1 The Culture of Lacrosse................................1
    Chapter 2 The Game and The People..........................33

Section 2 — The Continuing Education and Safety of All Participants
    Chapter 3 The Purpose and Vision of the Game...............59
    Chapter 4 The Art of Good Coaching and Officiating.........89

Section 3 — Sportsmanship and Character Development
    Chapter 5 Character Comes Alive................................117
    Chapter 6 Character and Lacrosse Performance............143

Section 4 — Responsible Administration and Commercialism
           for Lacrosse
    Chapter 7 Walking the Talk:
               Program and Team Management.................173
    Chapter 8 Marketing Lacrosse...................................183

Endgame — Next Steps...189

Index... 193
References 195
Resources 201

Foreword

Lacrosse originated centuries ago as an indigenous stickball game played by Native American tribes throughout the eastern half of North America. Today, the game has evolved to become one of the fastest growing sports in the United States and has spread to dozens of nations throughout the world.

Throughout much of the 20th century, lacrosse was known as little more than a regional oddity. In recent years, however, the popularity of the sport has reached Malcolm Gladwell's proverbial "tipping point" thanks, in large part, to equipment innovations, private sector investment, expanded promotional and development resources, and a national structure of leadership and administration.

The sport's new-found position of recognition and popularity, characterized by professional leagues, unprecedented media attention and ever-increasing private enterprise, has created both opportunities and challenges for lacrosse. The rules and equipment of lacrosse have evolved — as they must — but what of the sport's core values? Are they any less important than the goals of increased popularity and recognition?

When I was first exposed to lacrosse as a third-grader at Baltimore's St. Paul's School, the sport quickly captured my attention. St. Paul's has one of the richest lacrosse traditions of any secondary school in the country, but I never felt pressure to play. I also benefited greatly from the opportunity to play two other sports at St. Paul's – basketball and football – each of which provided me with different and equally beneficial experiences. Even at the University of North Carolina-Chapel Hill, where I was fortunate to play on teams that won consecutive national championships in 1981 and 1982, I never felt overwhelmed by the sport. Just about the time I started thinking about college choices – the summer before my senior year – the recruiting process began. But throughout that process, the anxiety I felt was generated by the importance of making the right educational choice. In the end I chose Carolina primarily because of the reputation of its School of Journalism, from which I received my undergraduate degree, not because of the reputation of its lacrosse program. In fact, at the time, UNC's lacrosse team had advanced to the NCAA tournament only once in its history. And, as a result of an unanticipated coaching change, I didn't meet my new college coach until my last high school lacrosse game...about 90 days before my first college classes began.

The lacrosse landscape has obviously changed dramatically over the last thirty years. The sport's growth has created a legitimate market that more and more people are trying to leverage into personal financial gain. A growing number of entrepreneurs have noted this trend and launched recruiting services, private club programs, camps and tournaments in unprecedented numbers. And, lured by the slight potential of reduced-priced tuition and admission consideration for their children, more and more parents are focusing on lacrosse as an anecdote for the rising cost of a college education. This growing financial motivation, along with a healthy dose of parental pride, have served as fuel for the growing trends we see in all youth sports today – sport specialization, poor sportsmanship, dishonesty, aggressive parental behavior, lapses in integrity and, ultimately, a negative sports experience for millions of young athletes. Sadly, the ultimate impact of these conditions is borne by the young athlete, who is becoming more of a commodity and whose sports experience is too often viewed as an investment toward an ultimate financial payoff. Is this trend an unavoidable bi-product of significant lacrosse growth? Should lacrosse take a stand to preserve the principles and values has so long represented?

These and other questions prompted US Lacrosse to launch an ambitious initiative called the *Campaign for Excellence*, the goal of which is to develop a comprehensive blueprint of our sport's culture – one that can be easily accessed and implemented by all program administrators so that the core values and traditions of lacrosse are always an important component of the lacrosse experience.

This book is a fundamental component of the *Campaign for Excellence*. John Yeager has gone to great lengths to uncover and clarify, through research, interviews and commentary, the heart and soul of our game. His thoughtful work will serve as a legacy that benefits lacrosse for generations to come. We're honored by John's contribution, by those who have contributed their thoughts and perspective to this work and, most importantly, by those of you who are committed to be culture keepers for our great game.

Steve Stenersen, Executive Director
US Lacrosse
October, 2005

Introduction

The nature of the game nurtures the soul of the player — Play with your heart and head — your body will follow — usually with positive results!
      —Jeff Long, Men's Head Coach, Ithaca College

Lacrosse had its beginnings on the pastures, fields and prairies of North America and has graduated to quick play on sleek synthetic turf. The game still resembles what seems like a rugby scrum of seven year olds going for a ground ball to the crisp transition of the ball traveling faster than a parent's eye operating a camcorder. This was and is lacrosse, a past time whose present time has arrived. The national governing body of lacrosse, US Lacrosse, has stepped up to take on the challenges of the rapidly growing game – to ensure that the past and present lead to a healthy future. Their credo speaks volumes to the challenge:

> *The mission of US Lacrosse is to ensure a unified and responsive organization that develops and promotes the sport by providing services to its members and programs to inspire participation, while preserving the integrity of the game. We envision a future that offers people everywhere the opportunity to discover, learn, participate in, enjoy, and ultimately embrace the shared passion of the lacrosse experience.*

The mission of US Lacrosse binds those involved in the game to a common purpose. As the whole is greater than the sum of its parts, it is essential that all stakeholder groups in all programs – players, coaches, administration, the industry, parents/spectators, and officials – "declare" themselves in following the mission and core values of US Lacrosse. Embracing core values symbolizes the shared commitment of each group to "One

v

Goal... Bringing Lacrosse to Life." Our game had for many years remained small enough to have avoided the serious conflict of values and actions that have affected sports larger than ours. As our sport continues to grow it is apparent now that all of us need to be proactive in promoting the values that attracted us to the sport and US Lacrosse in the first place. These values include: connection, leadership, respect, spirit, tradition, trust, and a commitment to youth.

By acting on and preserving the core values of the game, it gives each participant, at all levels, the greatest opportunity to be authentically happy and content. And the game ought to be about happiness and fulfillment. The ancient Greek philosopher Aristotle, never played the game, but his time-tested maxims are clearly marked in the game today – that a goal in life is to be happy. And happiness can come when people do things well. When lacrosse is played and coached the way it ought to be, then a level of excellence is attained – whether it be all-world, or a youth pick-up game. Erin Quinn, the men's head coach at Middlebury College, once said that lacrosse, in and of itself, means very little when you take the people out of the equation. It is the collaboration of players, coaches, parents, officials, athletic and program directors and other people in addition to the application of one's own efforts that brings meaning to the game. This is truly the aspiration to "authentic" happiness.

Martin Seligman, a pioneer in the field of positive psychology, believes that true happiness is based on three areas: the demonstration of positive emotion; the acquisition of positive character traits; and the influence of positive "institutions" on our behavior. These institutions include the kind of communities, families, schools and athletic programs in which we are involved. Happiness is not only about correctly executing X's and O's. It is about the people of the game – their experiences and stories that are handed down to succeeding generations of aspiring players and coaches. The stories of virtue in lacrosse have assisted us in becoming more knowledgeable and hopefully wiser as they have most certainly inspired belief and a sense of purpose within us. As we listen and have listened to the stories of our coaches, our players, our friends and teammates in the game, it is essential that we attend closely for the cues that uncover their beliefs and sense of purpose. By doing so, we are better able to empathize with their joys, elations, frustrations and troubles. This is where we can make a great difference in people's lives. The power of our stories can be quite riveting. When we tell lacrosse stories to others, not just for entertainment sake, we invite others to journey into the deeper gifts of the game. To tell a story is to possess someone in a way that a structured X and O game plan does not. As humans we desire to be "possessed" in that way on occasion. Learning how to make up, tell and even listen to a nuanced story is about balance and good judgment – the young players of today are hungry for that. These stories form the basis of the culture of our game and the character of those who participate in it.

Culture (kŭlchər) *n.* The totality of socially transmitted behavior patterns, acts, beliefs, institutions, and all other products of human work and thought characteristic of a community or population. A style of social and artistic expression peculiar to a society or class.

Char-ac-ter (kăr'a k-tər) *n.* The combined moral or ethical structure of a person or group. A description of a person's attributes, traits, or abilities.

Each section and chapter of the book addresses the US Lacrosse Standards for Excellence. Although this book provides strategies to build culture and character, it also asks the important questions of well-meaning and well-intentioned lacrosse partici-pants. These questions will help the reader reflect and make intentional choices about maintaining the integrity of the game.

In March 2005, I participated in US Lacrosse's first Cam-paign for Excellence Summit in Baltimore. I joined a variety of lacrosse enthusiasts from all constituencies to address and declare what matters most in the game. From these meetings, we were able to generate four "standards" that enable participants of the game to promote the core values of US Lacrosse and experience joy and satisfaction through their participation. The book is structured along the following criteria for excellence:

Standard 1: Maintain the Traditions and Culture of the Sport

Standard 2: Assure the Continuing Education and Safety of All Participants

Standard 3: Promote Sportsmanship and Character Development

Standard 4: Maintain Responsible Administration and Commercialism for Lacrosse

These "standards of excellence" are embedded in the text and are supported with a generous sampling of my own experiences and interview responses from various lacrosse participants. I have had the exciting opportunity to conduct a number of in-person, phone and email interviews with coaches, players, parents, officials, and administrators from all across the country. Also included are the results of a random sample survey of approximately 1,600 US Lacrosse members, who are involved with all levels of the game – from youth through post-collegiate lacrosse. Although we all have different desires and motives for our involvement in the game, we all have our stories. This book is a collection of stories, some that may ring familiar to you. Story-telling was and is still a trademark of the Native American tradition that provided roots to the game. It is my hope that the reader can transfer names to the coaches and players and other participants who have brought them a sense of enjoyment in the game.

Section 1 - The Traditions and Culture of the Sport

Preserving the integrity of lacrosse by honoring the past while bridging modern culture is one way to demonstrate respect

VIII

for the sport. The game then becomes a demonstration and expression of who we are on the field, providing each participant, at all levels, the greatest opportunity to aspire to authentic happiness. The culture of connection, as an example, bridges the American Indian with the American immigrant, as well as bridging generations and genders. The spirit is alive because these unique attributes exist in action as well as words.

Chapter 1 - The Culture of Lacrosse – The game of lacrosse has an embedded system of shared beliefs, values, customs, behaviors, and artifacts that have endured over time. Although the game grows and there are subtle changes in the culture, it is important to maintain the healthy values and traditions, the culture of lacrosse is changing. This chapter provides strategies that can be incorporated by becoming culture-keepers of lacrosse. An enduring question to ask is:

• How do we maintain the history and traditions of lacrosse within our program/team?

Chapter 2 – The Game and the People – This chapter examines how our connections with other people associated with the game may have inspired belief and a sense of purpose within us. An important question is:

• How do our associations with other lacrosse participants bring us enjoyment and satisfaction?

Section 2 – The Continuing Education and Safety of All Participants

Continuing education on the basic foundations of the game is critical for providing not only a safe but also, thriving, learning environment and a deeper appreciation of the sport. Strong leadership requires a commitment to providing quality guidance and instruction and a safe physical, emotional, mental, moral, and social climate for all participants. This commitment results in a knowledgeable lacrosse community and enables trust between participant groups - ensuring that people across the country are playing the same game, with the same rules and the same purpose.

Chapter 3 — The Purpose and Vision of the Game — Successful lacrosse programs are founded on a clear purpose for all involved. This chapter focuses on how our sense of purpose and meaning for participating in lacrosse reinforces our commitment to the game and enables trust between participant groups. The central questions are:

- How do the core values of lacrosse come alive in your program/team?
- What would you want other people to say about your program/team?
- Are your program/team core values in alignment with the ideal?

Chapter 4 — The Art of Good Coaching and Officiating — Good coaches and officials are mentors, modelers and managers for players. They share a strong purpose, are knowledgeable in the game, are relational in that all players and other participants matter, and have acquired a strong character. One question needs to be answered:

- What are the essential characteristics of "successful coaching and officiating" and what do these traits look like on and off the field?

Section 3 — Sportsmanship and Character Development

To truly commit to honoring the game of lacrosse, all participants must know what sportsmanship and positive character look like when they come alive on the field, and then demonstrate and celebrate them, beginning at the youth level. Sportsmanship is about developing positive habits so they become second nature. It is about behavior, and for some, about learning to change behavior. Just as the development of strong stick fundamentals requires countless hours on the wall, positive habits form when players, coaches, officials, administrators and spectators make serious and enduring efforts to act within the spirit of the game.

Chapter 5 – Character Comes Alive – Lacrosse coaches and parents of players are, by nature, character educators. When there is common ground among participants, the program sends a more consistent message to the athletes. This chapter examines how good character is embedded in the roots that are displayed in the perseverance of mastering stick fundamentals and developing a keen sense of game flow. Two questions are paramount:

- How do we see a player's "character formation" influenced by coaches, officials, parents and other important people at different levels of the game?
- How do you establish common ground with others on the definition of character habits?

Chapter 6 – Character and Lacrosse Performance – This chapter provides instruction on practical strategies that help link character habits to excellence on the field. One essential question is:

- How are your program/team's core values connected to performance on the field?

Section 4 – The Responsible Administration and Commercialism of Lacrosse

By recognizing the role and power to influence others, those responsible for the administration of lacrosse teams, leagues and clinics at all levels of the game and those who oversee the development, marketing and distribution of lacrosse products have a privilege and an opportunity to provide exemplary leadership. Responsible program administration and commercial marketing of products expands awareness for the sport, demonstrates a commitment to safety, and enables accessibility to the sport.

Chapter 7 — Walking the Talk — Program and Team Management — When coaches, parents, and administrators "walk the talk," their actions speak volumes to the players about the importance of doing lacrosse right. Program and team administrators figuratively, and sometimes literally "drive the bus." It is important to oversee and reinforce the program's mission. There is an important question for lacrosse administrators:

- Is the lacrosse program mission consistently carried out in your program?

Chapter 8 — Marketing Lacrosse — The growth of lacrosse has also spurned enormous development in the lacrosse industry. The industry is a prime stakeholder along with players, coaches, officials, parents and administrators in ensuring a quality experience for all participants. The profound questions are:

- How can the industry continue to develop marketable product in accordance with and consideration of the rules, safety and quality of the game?
- How does the industry market and value the culture of lacrosse?

Oliver Wendell Holmes, the notable poet and author, once said, "I would not give a fig (care) for the simplicity this side of complexity, but I would give my life for the simplicity on the other side of complexity." Translated in relationship to lacrosse, this quote states that "when lacrosse is done right" – and this may be up for discussion among different people with different motivations – the game is fairly simple. Once a player learns to catch and throw, a coach effectively translates important aspects of the flow of the game; officials communicate and adjudicate the letter and spirit of the rules, and parents understand the nuances of lacrosse, the game becomes quite simple. This simplicity then becomes the vehicle for joy and satisfaction – a source of true happiness. And isn't life about doing right for self and others to live a happy existence?

Whether you agree or disagree with all the tenets discussed in the following pages, try to see the big picture of the game and how all the dots connect. It is so important for the future of lacrosse. Nobody is bigger than the game and this contribution is merely one's attempt to give back to the sport of lacrosse. Our greatest gift is for us to be stewards of a game that has brought us enjoyment, satisfaction, and authentic happiness!

SECTION 1

The Traditions and Culture of the Sport

Chapter 1

The Culture of Lacrosse

*Our grandfathers told us that when lacrosse was a pure game and
was played for the enjoyment of the great spirit, everyone
was important, no matter how big or how small, or how
strong or how weak.*
—Tewaarthon; Akwesasne's Story of Our National Game

By honoring the past while bridging modern culture we
preserve the integrity of the game. The game then becomes a
demonstration and expression of who we are on the field, providing each participant, at all levels, the greatest opportunity to
aspire to authentic happiness. The culture of connection bridges
American Indians with American immigrants, as well as generations and genders.

From catgut sidewalls to offset heads, lacrosse's uniqueness
has established an enduring culture over the years. It is a sport
that all sizes and shapes and abilities can play. From the early
1970's and the creation of the plastic molded stick, we recapture
Hopkins' diminutive attackman Jack Thomas (5'3") passing to his
gigantic teammate Franz Wittlesberger (6'7"). Fast forward to the
new millennium and we capture the speed and flair of former
Maryland great and Team Australia's Jen Adams, her trademark
"buns" on top of her head, running at gazelle-like speed.

The game's richness has been founded on the premise that
the "whole is greater than the sum of its parts" – that the collaborative relationship of all the players on the field makes for successful
performance and overall satisfaction. As stated in the introductory

1

quote on the previous page, it is evident that the thrill of winning held not such an important role as did how the team played.

Culture and Change – Two Games One Goal

The game of lacrosse has an embedded system of shared beliefs, values, customs, behaviors, and artifacts that have endured over time. Although the game is rapidly growing and there are subtle changes in the culture, it is important to maintain the healthy values and traditions. However, at the same time, we need to work to incorporate what is new into an evolved tradition – one that we can be proud of and willingly hand off to our successors. As lacrosse becomes more complex, from the perspective of its participants' needs, wants, desires and motives, so does the need to preserve the rituals and stories surrounding it.

Lacrosse Culture "101"

People who are new to the game naturally bring culture and tradition from other sports to which they have been exposed. Although many parents and aspiring coaches have never played the game, they may have had experience in either playing and/or coaching other mainstream sports such as soccer, basketball or baseball/softball. Tony Seaman, men's head coach at Towson University, contends that a lot of parents who never played the game are parents of kids who do play the game and it is a carry over from one sport that the child plays to the next.

Erin Quinn, head men's coach at Middlebury College, never played lacrosse. His focus was on football until a serious injury ended his playing career at Middlebury. He had been fascinated watching his friends play lacrosse every spring, and he eventually became a student of the game under the tutelage of, then Middlebury head coach, Jim Grube. Erin would visit Jim in a "Breakfast Club" format every morning for two years as he learned the nuances of the game.

When I interviewed Dave Urick, head men's coach at Georgetown, there was a high school player in his office shadowing Dave as part of his local high school career project. This student eagerly participated in our discussion. His father had played at Maryland in the early 1980's. He mentioned that he was entranced with the wonderful story of "legacy of the stick" in Neil Duffy's book, *The Spirit in the Stick*. Duffy's deft storytelling can be compared with some themes in classical mythology such as *The Magic Talisman*, or when Arthur pulls the sword out in Excalibur, to more popular media such as the journey of Luke Skywalker. As Duffy states, the stick becomes an extension of oneself, of who we are. For coaches, this is something that we ought to communicate, if we aren't already, to the continuum of youth to elite players. Although today's technology affords players with sticks whose pockets may be pre-formed and ready to play, the stick is still the vehicle that makes the game happen. By sharing the nuances of stick work that influence mastery and performance, we share rich and meaningful aspects of the history, traditions and culture of this wonderful game.

Bowen Holden, former all-American goalie and head women's coach at Boston College, believes the mold of the game has changed over the years that she played. "As far as off the field, I don't feel that the culture has changed a whole lot in terms of the team aspect of it," she says. "I feel that being a part of the team has always been the same for me. It was the same whether I was on the soccer team or lacrosse team or now coaching. The lessons you learn and challenges you face are very much the same. If anything, culture changes the individual. You may have a different team culture because you have a different leader. Each year the team is different and the team forms to their personalities and their abilities and their goals."

John Pirani, head boys' coach at Winchester High School, MA, and the founder of Winchester's youth program, believes the challenge in evaluating any institution is recognizing that change is inevitable. Lacrosse is no exception. He claims, "Although many participants mourn change in the customization of stick technology or changes of field boundaries, they seldom recognize they are usually the agents of change. When we fall in love with something in this society, it seems that we want it to never change, but that is unrealistic. All things change and the key is to find what it is that we love in what is there. That doesn't mean we should accept a corrupted or contaminated version, but we do need to be pragmatic and understand how things morph."

Lacrosse seemed to stay the same for decades. In looking at sepia colored photos or wandering around the museum at US Lacrosse, people familiar with the game can easily see how little the game changed right up through the 1980's. For those that were involved pre-1980, it is tempting to cast all that is new as disrespectful of the traditions and history of the game. It is probably more accurate to note that those new to lacrosse are likely unaware of traditions rather than disrespectful. For the traditionalists, the key point is that those new to lacrosse cannot be judged as disrespectful of traditions. How can they be disrespectful if they don't know about lacrosse-focused traditions or the history of the game? If one accepts that change is inevitable, then inevitably, some of that change is going to be difficult for older stakeholders.

The history of lacrosse shows a remarkable evolution dating back literally hundreds of years. The stakeholders have changed slowly but dramatically over time. As those changes naturally happen, the values of the people and elements of lacrosse that their predecessors found attractive may not be so important any longer. In and of itself, this is not a problem, certainly in modern times; many have played, coached and watched lacrosse for their own and different reasons. Sleights toward the history of the game, I think, are mostly not intended as sleights. It is usually just people approaching the world as they always have and that is usually without any bad intentions.

In working with a group of youth coaches, many who had played as kids, John Pirani noted that there was a need to ensure that sportsmanship and camaraderie remain central to the younger player's experiences. A few of the coaches felt those characteristics should go unstated as they had never been a part of a team that didn't live sportsmanship and have a wonderful feeling for teammates. In the end, however, the group decided that nothing should be taken for granted. The consensus was that as lacrosse grew, many more people without a common background in the game have come to play with sensibilities from other sports; sports that may not value the traditions of lacrosse. That is, there was a real concern that values associated with sport in general would overcome those traditionally associated with lacrosse.

Erin Quinn believes the game is obviously expanding and has gone from a provincial sport to a national sport. It has lost a lot of its parochial flavor; however, some of that can be a good thing because the benefits of the game can be brought to people in Tennessee, California, Utah, Texas and other states. Lacrosse is a predominantly amateur sport and almost has a club feel to it. "One of the interesting things about the future of lacrosse is its growth from the bottom up. It is like a pyramid with an enormous base and a little pinprick at the top. If pro lacrosse and Division I lacrosse are at the top of the pyramid, it is so small as compared to the growing foundation," says Quinn.

A dramatic fact is that lacrosse has changed in terms of how people are now introduced to the game. For those who have been involved in the game for years, there is a celebration of the legacy and the continual quest for keeping lacrosse as pure as possible. Lacrosse is at a crossroads today – a re-evolution of both the women's and men's games to seek one goal in preserving the culture and traditions. As US Lacrosse anticipates membership of up to 190,000 enthusiasts in 2006, how can we best blend the past and the present, and anticipate the future to make game the best it can be? Some worry some about the direction of the game. Its growth is both a blessing and a curse. As lacrosse gets bigger, the demand for the involvement of more people who are not schooled in the tradition and history challenges the legacy of the game. If the strength lies in the tradition and the character of the game, how do we convey that to young players when those coaching it never learned it themselves?

Communicating and Honoring the Legacy of Lacrosse

When I interviewed Sid Jamieson, a Native American who recently retired after 40 years as the head men's coach at

Bucknell, he acknowledged the importance of lacrosse participants' understanding the roots of the game. Jamieson believes that young players are hungry to listen to and imagine how the game evolved from its roots. He says, "I continue to do the talks at all the camps I do during the summer. You could hear a pin drop when we are giving these talks to the kids. And I will get back to campus and I will get a phone call, or a letter, or an email from a parent, who said 'You know, my son came back and said he enjoyed the camp – he is a changed person, in a certain sense, because of the talk that you presented at the camp.' I have heard that consistently over the years. I think it is important. I think the kids do really want to hear it. They don't hear it anywhere else."

When Coach Jamieson speaks of the legacy and myth of the game, he communicates as oral storytelling. Many years ago, myth was tied to religion, as were the sacred narratives of our Native American forebearers. To read the stories of the evolution of lacrosse, you would see the use of "animals" as metaphors for people. This is a pre-cursor to modern sports, as many teams have mascots based on "predatory" and powerful animals – Bears, Falcons, Tigers, etc. In many ways, these stories represent a "sacred narrative" that operates at two levels: it is cultural – the values of the culture that produced the narrative; and it is universal – tells something about human traits, and crosses time and space. In other words, myth addresses what it means to be human. Unfortunately, as there has been a breakdown in aspects of American culture, so to has there been a breakdown of mythology and traditions. Rollo May, the legendary Harvard philosopher, writes about the "cry for myth" as a means for the values of the culture to be displayed, and to tell participants something about human traits that cross time and space. In other words, myth and tradition address what it means to be human. For example, rules and time outs in the game and the use of primary colors by pre-modern athletic teams all grew out of myth.

Both John Piper, head boys' coach at North Carroll High School, MD, and I realized that the players on our respective teams called our fastest player "deer." I never thought this stuff connected with the kids until I started an end-of-season tradition with my Culver team. At our last practice of every season, I read several passages from "Tewaarthon," a wonderful book published by the North American Indian Traveling College in Upstate New York. Following the passage, the players share some thoughts about each of the graduating seniors. Immediately after this, the seniors walk, one by one, through a "tunnel" of crossed sticks held above the returning underclassmen. This ritual is always a powerful experience for the players and coaches.

Jamieson believes what really makes the connection is when a young person is introduced to the game and has some basic knowledge of its history. He claims it is both challenging and interesting to be able to dream about what the game really was like in the old days between villages playing 20-30 miles in distance, with huge ceremonies. This may sit nicely in the back of their minds – a little dream about this real game. Then you connect it with the physicality of the game of lacrosse, which can be an individual dream. There is such a uniqueness about the game of lacrosse and open spaces and running and being able to express yourself out there, which is in essence, what the game is really all about. It's about an opportunity for all players to express themselves. It is an opportunity to express who they are out on the field. While young people may not understand that this is happening, in reality, that is what they are doing.

Honoring the Past – Playing in the Present

If we respect and honor the past, which is history, it becomes a whole lot more than just the game. It becomes a demonstration of who we are when we are out there playing. So, if you understand the historical part of this, and if you put that into a proper perspective, then it's not just a game anymore. It's really an expression of your own personal parts, all of your parts – as you go out there and begin to play the game. That's what the history is and that's the way the game should be played.

— Sid Jamieson, Former Head Men's Coach,
Bucknell University

Alan McCoy, head boys' coach and athletic director at The Pingree School in Hamilton, MA, grew up in Western New York and played for the legendary Hall of Famer and Tuscarora Indian, Wes Patterson. While Alan was in school, Wes was making sticks; steaming and bending the crosse, drilling holes, and weaving the pocket and the gut wall. He custom-made every stick Alan used in high school. He also shared ceremonial dances with the players at Kenwood during athletic retreats. Alan remembers Wes as a fabulous storyteller, a great coach and above all a kind, humorous individual who treated every player with care and dignity. This tradition has been passed down to a small camp McCoy runs for kids during the summer. "We open each session with the story of the game. It is amazing to see eight, nine and ten year olds so engrossed in the telling. It is not something I have experienced in any other sport.

"It's the respect for the rules and playing the game to honor the game that amazes me," says Dee Stephan, head coach at Avon High School, CT and the US Lacrosse Connecticut Chapter president. "We do not necessarily recognize the Native American traditions but the traditions of the women's game: fair play, honesty, respect for your opponent and the umpires are all part of the tradition we embrace. I also see players embracing the beauty of a play of another player's goal or a team's fast break, recognizing it for its beauty."

The results of a survey, administered to a critical mass of US Lacrosse members, are shared within the text. The original roll-out was a random sampling of 1,6000 US Lacrosse members — players, coaches, officials, parents, administrators, and the lacrosse industry, who support and are involved with all levels of the game — from youth through post-collegiate lacrosse. The results of this survey are embedded in the book and reflect what is being said about today's game. The survey captures the similarities and differences of how each participant views "what matters most" in the game.

Ninety percent of those surveyed agree that the history and traditions of lacrosse are very important to the modern game.

Survey of Lacrosse Stakeholders

The history and traditions of lacrosse are very important to the modern game.

		Number of Responses	Response Ratio
Strongly Agree	�	*642*	*41%*
Agree	▬	*776*	*49%*
Disagree	▪	*151*	*10%*
Strongly Disagree	▪	*11*	*1%*
	Total	*1580*	*100%*

The Culture within the Culture

Every team and every lacrosse program has its own sub-culture. There are certain nuances, norms and expectations that have been established over time that create the culture. This can be incredibly positive or disappointingly negative.

Chris Paradis, head women's head coach at Amherst College, has worked hard to build a team culture that is very familial. Respect for one another by demonstrating a real love for one another and for the game has made the "Lady Jeffs" an attractive program. Chris sets high expectations for her players. In her first years, she had to explain training rules off the field and other important foundations to establish a good program. Over time, however, the younger players have learned what it is to be a part of the program by the modeling and dialogue of older players who help instill a passion for the game.

Another prime example of the importance of team culture is provided by Greg Cannella, head men's coach and former player at the University of Massachusetts. "When I came back to coach in fall of 1992, there was a vastly different culture than the present day. That is not to say we have more or less talent – that is hard to measure. However, I feel we have changed the approach that players take during the process of a season and their careers. With competition as it is and the exposure the sport receives, it is a very different world. I have always tried to stress the importance of working your hardest, and giving your best day in and day out! I often ask 'what do you want out of this?' – in an attempt to make these student-athletes think about themselves and why they do what they do."

The change in culture at UMass really emerged in 1999 when one of their players, Eric Sopracasa passed away. Cannella says that this event "really woke the guys up." It took a tragic experience like that to really get the attention and focus of the players to find out what is the cause of their charge. "We hold Eric in such high regard," Greg said, "for what he stood for and the energy and power he brought to us. That energy and power transformed many of these guys into men with great focus and attention to doing their best. We have carried Eric's legacy with us and continue to talk about what his legacy means to our program. We still honor him with an Eric Sopracasa Award - Heart and Soul Award – given to the player or players who represent his legacy the best. We want everyone to have the over-achieving, tenacious attitude Eric possessed, along with being a great teammate and friend on a daily basis, as he was."

Bridging the Roots of Women's Lacrosse – Past to Present

It is easy to acknowledge and celebrate tradition at Bryn Mawr because there is something almost poetic about the fact that the high school game came from this school. Roosevelt Sinclair, a pioneering icon of women's lacrosse, taught and coached here. The roots of the game are here at this school and the inaugural woman's game to be played in the United States was Bryn Mawr vs. Friends School in 1926 on a field that the school now owns. We have had t-shirts made, screened with *Bryn Mawr Lacrosse Established 1926.* This is a big deal and many of the girls really understand the importance of those who came before them.

— Wendy Kridel, Head Coach, Bryn Mawr;
  U.S. Women's Head Coach - Under 19

There is another vibrant culture twenty miles down the road from UMass at Springfield College. Keith Bugbee's abundance of lacrosse alums are referred to as the "Springfield Mafia." Many have gone into coaching at either the college or high school level. Bugbee exclaims that, "Many guys giving back to the game by becoming coaches is wonderful. I really feel it's the most rewarding part of my job."

Gene Zanella, head boys' coach at Framingham High School, MA, recalls a recent comment from a player who explained why he liked lacrosse better than football, "Football is an activity that I play; lacrosse is like a part of who I am." Zanella speaks further to this point, "I will not say all my athletes feel this way, but many of our players feel lacrosse influences their life in many ways. Many students develop a life-long commitment to the sport of lacrosse. They do not leave it behind as they leave high school. I am always amazed at the number of former players that remain committed to the game as players or coaches."

The Re-Evolution of Lacrosse

Both the men's and women's games have experienced extraordinary growth over the past decade as seen in significant membership increase at the youth level, the emergence of "pay for play" club programs, the dramatic increase in summer camp opportunities, media exposure, and stick and other equipment technology. We are experiencing a trend in specialization in both games and significant changes in the field boundaries in the women's game. It is interesting to note that there was great consistency among those interviewed in what they believe to be important factors in the lacrosse re-evolution.

The Emergence of Youth Lacrosse—
Responsibilities, Challenges and Opportunities

Over the past 15 years, youth lacrosse has boomed in the United States. To date, the overwhelming majority of US Lacrosse memberships belong to youth players. They are the future of the game. The emergence of this phenomenon, however, has also created many challenges.

Jay Williams, head of the Massachusetts Bay Youth Lacrosse League (MBYL), remembers the spring of the 1993 season when they started off with 13 towns which involved 400 young players. As of 2004, there were 105 towns with boys' program and an explosion of 40-50 towns with girls' teams in the MBYL. This includes 9,000 boy and 4,500 girl participants. Age groups have gone down to Under 11. Some towns have gone to intramural or house leagues and some out-of-town travel teams, and have also widened their span to Under 9 programs. Williams sees a natural progression to high school lacrosse with around 100 towns that now have varsity programs.

Gene Zanella suggests that youth coaches have important responsibilities as positive role models. However, the time of contact with these athletes is much less when compared to high school coaches. High school coaches will spend 15 to 20 hours per week while youth coaches will spend 5 to 8 hours a week with the athlete. The opportunity for a youth coach to influence an athlete's character can be magnified for the athlete who falls in love with the game of lacrosse because he or she will follow the example set by the coach.

Peter Lasagna, head men's coach at Bates College, believes that the youth coaches' role is paramount to the success of the youth player. He has seen that many young players tend not to be as patient in learning the game. They want immediate gratification. At the same time, less parents of youth players are supportive of coaching decisions. Accountability and responsibility has really changed. Therefore, the youth coach becomes a primary stake-holder in the appropriate development of the youth player.

The Club — "Pay for Play" Experience

Jay Williams suggests the latest challenge for MBYL and other youth programs is that you can hold so many people at bay for so long under the current constitution. Select teams are popping up all over the place with A, B, and C tiers. The "pay for play" phenomena in lacrosse is gaining momentum as seen in a number of select, elite programs being offered throughout the country. For the administrators providing these programs, there may be competing motivations regarding the economic and educational benefits of the business. Parents of youth involved ought to ask these administrators two important questions prior to signing up: "What is it that you offer my child? and How will I know that you have fulfilled this obligation?" Some "pay for play" programs hold shallow promises when declaring that your son or daughter will be recruited by Division 1 college programs. It is vitally important that parents are well-informed by reading the fine print and making a decision that is in the best interests of their child or children.

Wendy Kridel, head girls' coach at The Bryn Mawr School, MD, is one of the "purists" who is trying to find an answer to the important question: "How do you grow with the times and still hold on to what you really believe in?" She is often asked questions by parents about their daughters — "What should I do with her? Where should I send her to play club? Does she need to do this? You are trying to advise parents and as much as I want to be able to say, 'Oh, no, your daughter doesn't need to play on a club team.' I can't because if they really are serious about trying to play in college it is very hard." She admits that college coaches are very busy and it is difficult for them to get out to see high school teams play. They will watch a video tape and listen to a call from the high school coach for a "blue-chip" recruit. But there also is the adolescent player who can afford to go play every weekend in all these tournaments – and she may not be the marquee player from their high school program. Wendy poses two other important questions: "Are we getting away from high school sports altogether? Are we going to find ourselves in a club format, and how much do these kids have to specialize?"

Coach Kridel also sees the positive side of the club pro-grams. "There are kids where you can see that it works because they are not into the social scene as much. One of the greatest benefits of club situations is that players really do get to form great relationships with kids that are not in their own school. They get to know them first as an athlete and begin to form this great bond as they spend a lot of time together. It is not just when they are out on the field, but also, when they are sitting under the tent eating, like snacking after the games. The parents get to meet each other, too. That part of it is really great for the girls."

Some adolescents don't know how to set limits on their many athletic commitments. Coach Kridel talks to parents and encourages them to be a filter, not an enabler. When the child is constantly on the go and the parent continues to drive her everyplace to play, then there isn't going to be a change in behavior. This pattern can risk injury and possibly burnout. Kridel has this conversation with her players' parents prior to the season. However, there are those that thrive on the "busyness." They can handle the academic rigor and can play all of the sports because they are willing to give up the party scene. Lacrosse becomes their social life.

Ricky Fried, head women's coach at Georgetown, says that one of the cultures that has changed is the club aspect of women's lacrosse. "This has changed dramatically in the last three to five years. One feels that they need to be part of a club team to go on to the next level and to be seen. It started out to be league teams to give high level kids an opportunity to play with each other against other high level teams. There is clever marketing being done to have everybody sign on to a club team for a lot of different reasons. Some may do it because of college coaches, some are the people making money through this and also the kids are playing all year around, which I don't necessarily think is a great thing either. We look for players who play other sports and enjoy other sports. They have other perspectives on things and end up wanting to play for us, as opposed to feeling like it's just another job."

Summer Camps

Summer lacrosse camps are emerging all around the country. The March issue of Lacrosse Magazine perennially features the plethora of camps that extend from Maine to Hawaii.

Camp listings range from individual to team camps (a high school team goes as a group) to a variety of positional/specialty, and those for beginners to advanced skills. Lacrosse Magazine's display of the camps asks the vendors to include their "mission statement and strengths of the camp" in the listing. Many camps uphold their mission and provide a meaningful experience, whether it is working on fundamentals, very competitive games or a blend of both. Some camps, however, have a "meat market" mentality and will take as many campers as there are beds and fields. There is little concern with staff/camper ratio, and in the long run, the campers' overall experience. Again, parents should be good filters and ask the important questions of camp administrators, who in turn, ought to ask themselves – "Are we doing what we say we are doing? If the answer is yes, then we've got a good camp going!"

Peter Lasagna recalls some thoughts of Jim Fritz' that were in a past *Inside Lacrosse* magazine article. "As a baby boomer, almost everybody you know that is close to our age realizes that a big part of how we learned the game and how we were taught to think about it, we learned it through working lacrosse camps – it is how you got yourself out there. People got to know who you were and they helped to develop future coaches. With very few exceptions, that is not what lacrosse camps are about now. The function is about exposure and recruiting from the player, parent and coaches side, and so it is going to be very interesting to see how it impacts the game. So much of how the culture has been handed down, regardless of the correct way to execute a roll dodge or a ten man ride, is missing. In the last five years, to a large part, this has been eliminated."

Erin Quinn claims that some of these pressures with summer camp recruiting and off season recruiting come from the game's growth. As there is a premium on spots at the tiny top of the pyramid, there is more competition for those five guys who want to be noticed. There is a prevailing understanding that it is not good enough to be seen on a high school tape or have a high school coach calling anymore. You have got to be seen at the top camps early on.

So What? – Educating New Coaches and Officials

Your coach was, and still is in some cases, the person who transferred the gift of the origins of the game to you. However, today young players have so many coaches, especially those who play in a "12 month" cycle. The message is delivered to youth in so many different ways by different people, and this can be confusing. There is a need for more education, adult training, and in many instances, a re-education. However, the education of new coaches and officials is no easy task. It is important to teach new coaches and officials that the values and traits of the North American's Indian roots basically run parallel with the things that we want the kids to know in the game - It's a natural. Some new coaches will ask: "Why do I need to know this? This is a game with players, goals, balls, sticks and a field. These are the rules. I am transfer-ring over my understanding of other sports and I am going to coach these kids to the best of my ability." We need to be better at helping stakeholders understand the <u>why</u> as much as the how.

> Lacrosse coaching has combined this incredible gift for passing on this game we are so deeply connected to: Sharing the uniqueness of the game's "spirituality" and its connection to the first Americans – the North American Indians. That is an amazing phenomenon to me. Does it make us better people? Not necessarily, but it makes us aware of people that came before us. This allows us to honor those people which is something that is very special. Other sports do that, but not with the richness in history that lacrosse provides.
> — Peter Lasagna, Head Men's Coach at Bates College

Jay Williams believes that the tradition of the game has been diluted since his introduction back in the early 1970's. He remarks that this explosion of success has legs of its own and, unfortunately sends the message that people do not necessarily have to give back to the game because it has its own momentum with it being played in all three seasons. Some parents who are new to the game may ask, "What's the big deal with honoring culture and tradition? My son or daughter has the equipment, knows the rules, and just goes out and does it on the field. I know how other sports are played. This is a logical transition over to lacrosse. Thanks for the lecture on the 'roots' of the game, but this is 2005 and we have no time for a history lesson. Everything is happening in the here and now and we have to get it done."

Passing on the tradition and culture of the game through stories provides an invitation to hear and tell our stories. No one is bigger than the game. It is the people that make lacrosse come alive including new coaches and officials.

Specialization – Is More Lacrosse Better?

As the game has grown there has been a trend in specialized positions at the college and even high school levels. The specialization takes a different perspective at the youth and high school level with a dramatic increase in young people who have decided to focus on lacrosse as their sport.

Positional Specialization

Dave Urick, head men's coach at Georgetown, member of the National Lacrosse Hall of Fame, and author of nine NCAA Division III championships at Hobart, knows the game. He claims that we are so focused on the game now, especially in the specialized aspects of the game. Several years ago you didn't see as much specialization. The positions of short stick defensive midfielder and the FOGO – (face off, get off the field) have evolved. Division I teams now have an assistant coach who just runs the substitution box. The box is, more than ever, becoming an important part of game strategy – trying to get players on and off the field as efficiently as possible. "As coaches, particularly at top end of Division I, we have a pretty firm grip on the game and, sometimes, maybe more than we should. Some of today's most recognized coaches, such as Bill Tierney at

Princeton and Dave Pietramala at Johns Hopkins, have really changed the men's game with their forward thinking ideas about defense play," said Urick. "That is an evolution of the game growing in popularity and growing in stature and the coaches have become a lot more sophisticated in their approach."

Rob Quinn, head men's coach at Colby College, claims the popularity and growth of lacrosse has changed the culture of the game and the way it is played. He believes that athleticism and speed have replaced size and physical play. Gone are the days of the two-way rugged midfielder, the huge crease attackman that nobody could move and that physical defender who placed fear in attackman's eyes. The game has become specialized by position and is dictated by possessions. The days of "run and gun" and scores in the high teens have now been replaced by low scoring affairs in the single digits that are won by defenses and face-off men. These thoughts are echoed by Matt Palumb, a former All-American goalie at Syracuse who recently refereed the 2005 NCAA Division I Men's championship game. He says the big challenge in officiating is "keeping up with the speed of the game." Players are bigger, faster and stronger, with advanced weight training and cardiovascular conditioning programs a staple of schools that want to be competitive.

Sport Specialization

John Pirani and his assistant coaches encourage all of their players to compete in at least one other sport during the school year. "We want those boys to play without the pressure of feeling like they are missing something," he says. "Winter youth clinic in the field house starts in January so we can work on the idea of coaching the coaches as our high school players lead drills and begin to hone their coaching skills and build relationships with younger players."

Chris Paradis mentions a conversation she had with a parent of a six year old regarding off-season lacrosse. Chris suggested to the parent that her child ought to be exposed to one activity at a time. No need to be working on a sport in the off season. Even with the dual sport athletes, the other sport is so valuable. What you learn in one sport can transfer to another. There is a confidence and resiliency that you can build from participating in different activities.

Erin Quinn says, "In the town of Middlebury, we will have some indoor youth tournaments for kids so they have a chance to play in the fall. That means that they are not playing soccer, not playing field hockey or not playing football. At the College, we are still able to encourage two sport athletes. I still coach two sports and I like it. I think that the involvement that they have in other things is a good, positive thing. We have become a first choice sport where as ten or fifteen years ago we would have some football players that would play lacrosse. Now we have lacrosse players that might play football. When they come to Middlebury, they may choose not to play football anymore. They want to specialize in lacrosse. I would like to teach the kids that playing two or three sports in high school and being involved in other things is a benefit to their lacrosse experience. It's fun. There is a lot to gain from other sports and even as a lacrosse player I think that the guy who has played in different sports sees things differently, more broadly."

Kate Dresher and Abby Burbank see youth lacrosse's growth in Colorado as another wonderful opportunity for rounding out the "whole person." They were quoted by Alex Wolff in a 2005 *Sports Illustrated* article: "They do a lot of things – ski, snowboard, hike – and lacrosse allows for that."

Paul Schimoler, head men's coach at St. Michael's College in Vermont and two-time U.S. National Team goalie, is very cautious about the growth and specialization of the game. He laments his case in "The Lost Season."

The Lost Season

Lacrosse has lost its "season". It has gained spice and flavor, but there is one flavor very few can taste anymore. The flavor many remember as the taste of the "lacrosse season" is diluted by the

continued on next page...

... continued from previous page

year round abundance of lacrosse. I love the game and the tremendous growth it has seen over the past decade. However, the sweetness of anticipation for the snow to thaw and the grass to green has been lost to the incessant foreplay of lacrosse year round.

Growing-up on Long Island there was lacrosse, but nothing like it is now. You would sign-up for youth leagues in February, start playing in March until school was over and then is was summer. Maybe there was a camp you would or could go to. Now, you have hundreds of camps to choose from. Recruiting camps, shooting camps, goalie only camps, defense camps, Top-this camp, Top-that camp, it goes on and on.

What did we do in the off-season? Soccer, football, basketball, hockey, racquet sports, wrestling, relaxing, learning, growing, being an athlete… A time to explore, imagine and create. Creating hybrid sports that were connected to lacrosse were my favorite. Hybrids like playing stickball with the pitcher throwing with a lacrosse stick and batting a tennis ball with a broom handle. Like playing one-on-one and two-on-two lacrosse in the shallow end of the pool with mini-lacrosse sticks, construction horses as goals and old bed sheets for a net. I liked to change it up! How about throwing a lacrosse ball with your bare hand and catching it with a baseball mitt?

I learned so much while playing different sports and "hybrid sports". I learned how to cut back door while playing two-on-two hoops. I learned how to throw a "pitch" with my stick to the outside corner of the strike zone. I learned how to save and catch the infield grounder to prevent the "single". I love lacrosse, but I also enjoyed and learned from other sports and "hybrids". It was different and creative and it was FUN!

—Paul Schimoler, Head Men's Coach, St. Michael's College

Jennifer Waldron, from the Institute for the Study of Youth Sports at Michigan State University, says, "Most people agree that sport provides many benefits, such as cooperation, skill development, teamwork, and fitness, for youth participants. In recent years, many parents, coaches, and athletes have felt the pressure for youth sport participants to specialize in order to be successful. Specialization or year-round involvement of youth in one particular sport, at the expense of playing multiple sports, however, may not provide the expected benefits and may be harmful in the long run."

We are starting to see a trend in sport specialization by younger athletes, which also includes lacrosse. With the advent of indoor facilities that offer lacrosse, we see children and adolescents playing the game year round, and in a growing number of cases, young people choosing to specialize in lacrosse at a very young age.

Equipment Technology – The Stick

The lacrosse stick still is truly an extension of a player's body that allows an individual to express and demonstrate skill development. Although there are hockey sticks, and baseball and softball bats that serve as fundamental equipment in their respective sports, the outcomes of a pass, catch, shot or check can be modified to a greater degree by the lacrosse player. The more skilled one becomes, the greater the opportunity to free the player up to have more options with his or her stick.

Players continue to ask me what kind of stick they should purchase. I always tell them to buy a "lacrosse stick." They looked at me in bewilderment waiting for the punch line and my anointing the right stick for them. Should they have an "offset" head – now that is standard with most every stick. Although stick technology has radically changed and is big business now, wooden sticks seem to be ancient history, except for the great tradition that Kathy Jenkins has at St. Agnes/St. Stephens in Virginia. Roy Simmons, Jr., who won six national championships while coaching as Syracuse University, once told me that Alfie Jacques, from a great stickmaking family of Mohawks in Nedrow, New York, now only makes around five dozen sticks a year – mostly to be sold as gifts.

The Stick

The thing that attracted me to the sport of lacrosse was very much the history of the game and the roots of the game. When I started playing lacrosse at Brown, I had heard of the game, but hadn't seen it. Even though I had no background in the game I had a great experience because you were playing with the best freshman in the class. We were all in the same group and you were given a chance to develop, especially in the first year. I was a history major at Brown and always had an interest in history and, to be honest, I became fast friends with Dave White, who is a Mohawk Indian who still lives on the St. Regis reservation. I was absolutely fascinated with the native American roots of the game. I spent some time early in my career on the Reservation playing box lacrosse and I loved the game at that level. I was absolutely fascinated with the stick. I loved working with the lacrosse stick. I quickly learned how to string my own sticks. My lacrosse stick, at the risk of melodrama, became my best friend in a lot of ways. That to me is a part of the game that I'm afraid we're losing - being in touch with the history of the game and then also the kids growing up with a fascination for their first stick. It was so important for me to get better as a stick handler – playing on the wall, learning how to play the game the right way. In some ways, I feel like children are a little bit more attracted to the glamour of the game and not so much to the historical roots of it, and that would be a shame.

—Dom Starsia, Head Men's Coach, University of Virginia

Tony Seaman, head men's coach at Towson University, says, "The one thing that I loved about lacrosse from the first time I became involved was that the little kid could play, the big kid could play, the slow and fat, the kid who had no spine could avoid the tough ground ball, he could avoid the big defensemen who beat up everybody and could still play the game pretty effectively. Practice was fun. Just taking the stick out to the back wall, and throwing against it. It allowed you to see if you were better in an hour. You could practice it by yourself or with somebody. You had a tool, a piece of equipment that became real personal, and that could shape and mold and do things with. When we first started, we had wooden sticks. When they broke, you would drill little screws into the wood, re-tape the fiberglass taping and then learn to sand it down and be ready to play again."

Media and Commercialism of Lacrosse

Tony Seaman suggests that three cultural changes stand out: news media coverage, television coverage, and internet coverage. They allow the game to be shown to people who have never seen the game. ESPN has committed to the NCAA Division I Men's championships and provided many lacrosse novices with their first view of the game, such as the exciting one-goal 2004 championship game between Syracuse and Navy. A variety of people, who had no clue about the game prior to Memorial Day Weekend, 2004, came up to me and said that the championship game was one of the most exciting sports events they had every witnessed. They all commented on the speed and quickness of the action.

The internet has also had a big effect. On the internet, you can say whatever you want to say and not have to take any responsibility for it. Players, parents and fans can log on to chat rooms and speak their mind. It's hard to stay off of the internet – it brings up a certain amount of emotion. Of course, we don't want to oppose our first amendment rights to free speech, but a caustic remark on a site that attacks the character, skills and overall credibility of a player or coach can be interpreted in ways which an in-person dialogue or phone conversation doesn't. The league that my high school team is in started a similar chat room. Part way through the season, I received an email from the league president, informing me that several of my players, who had clandestine passwords, were forbidden from continuing on the site. I confronted these young men, and before I could communicate my disappointment on how they were representing our school in public, they quickly mentioned they were just responding to inflammatory remarks from members of other teams. The important question to ask: Is this good for the game, even within an evolving culture. Some adults would say – these are just kids being kids. You make the call!

Roy Simmons, Jr. told me, "In all the years of *Sports Illustrated*, there has only been one lacrosse player on the cover." *SI* felt that their magazine was nationwide, and why would they publish something that wasn't of interest other than in small pockets of the Northeast, so they turned their back on lacrosse. However, that might be changing. Hence a nine-page *Sports Illustrated* article on the sport's growth in 2005. Simmons goes on to say, "It is an American sport. Another thing I saw grow, lacrosse wasn't as popular until it came on television. When I was coaching in the late 80's, I can remember bringing my team to a national championship in Maryland and national TV was there. However, they didn't know how to film it and how to broadcast it. And I had to sit down with the broadcaster. He was told to broadcast this lacrosse game on Memorial Day, but he didn't know too much about the game. They did it because they had to do it, not because they wanted to do it. Eventually ESPN picked it up and brought it into living rooms all around the country. That has helped the game a lot. It's going to take television contracts to make the United States aware of what a wonderful game it is!"

The lacrosse industry has kept up with the growth of both the men's and women's games. Each vendor is in direct competition with the others to produce the best equipment for the huge market, which includes the youth cohort. There has been a great amount of controversy and discussion about the roles and responsibilities of the lacrosse industry in conforming to the foundational standards of the game. Traditionalists and purists are sickened by the sexy ads in catalogs, web sites, and at booths. Others claim it is just another way to promote the game.

Marc Van Arsdale, assistant men's coach at Virginia, sees a transformation in the culture of the game as a result of the change in sticks and product development. It is no longer just

Brine or STX. Now with so many vendors, it speaks again to the growth of the game and the commercialization piece. You would hope that it has made the play of the game better in some ways.

Cultural Changes in Women's Lacrosse

The women's game is based upon players' speed and finesse rather than the deliberate body to body and stick to body contact. In my opinion, women's lacrosse showcases women's athletic ability more than any other game women play. Played well the game is like ballet with sticks in players' hands.
  —Susie Ganzenmuller, Women's Official,
    2005 National Lacrosse Hall of Fame Inductee

Women's lacrosse, with its first game in 1926, has experienced substantial growth in numbers in the past decade. As play has adapted, a hybrid stick fundamental style from the men's side, stick technology, and the use of goggles are part of the re-evolution of the game. There also have been substantive rule changes and new philosophies about field boundaries. Pat Dillon, chair of US Lacrosse's executive committee, and a leading women's official, claims that the women's game is at a crossroads in its enormous growth, with the need to bring in new coaches and officials while retaining more experienced coaches and officials. Missy Foote, head women's coach at Middlebury College, suggests that the culture of women's athletics in the last 30 years has changed since the advent of Title IX. There are more women playing all sports in both high school and college.... and lacrosse in particular. Lacrosse was a sport that was added to many universities in order to comply with Title IX. Foote says, "The rules of the women's game have changed tremendously with societal norms and in response to the skills of women getting better - women getting stronger and faster, and new plastic sticks allowing the ball to be passed and shot harder. In the early 70s checking was only allowed from the front."

> *The "freedom" of lacrosse also makes it special — the ability*
> *to run with your head up (no ball on the ground)*
> *makes it feel unbridled and joyful.*
>
> —Missy Foote, Head Women's Coach, Middlebury College

According to Coach Foote, it has become very cool now for middle school and high school girls to play lacrosse. She says, "Jen Adams from Maryland wore her hair in a bun and now lots of high school players are wearing their hair in buns as well. So, there is a media role model for women in lax."

In women's lacrosse there are positions on the field for almost every type of player. A fast girl can play midfield and be successful with very few stick skills; a big, slower girl can play low defense or low offense and be successful; and a quick agile, smaller player can play high attack and be good. Kate Dresher, executive director of the Colorado Lacrosse Foundation and current president of the US Lacrosse Youth Council, emphasizes the importance of the growing the game from the bottom. Young girls have enthusiasm and passion at an early age. To bring this interest and eagerness to a sport that is different than the typical mainstream sports invites opportunities for challenge and satisfaction.

From United States Women's Lacrosse Association to US Lacrosse

The spirit of the women's game continues to be based upon players' speed and finesse rather than deliberate body to body and stick to body contact. Susie Ganzenmuller, a 2005 inductee into the National Lacrosse Hall of Fame says, "Women's lacrosse showcases a women's athletic ability more than any other game women play. Played well, the game is like ballet with sticks in players' hands." Her thoughts resonate with me back to the early 1990's when I spent part of the season as a sport psychology consultant with the Harvard's women's team, under the tutelage of the legendary Carol Kleinfelder. Being versed in the men's game, I was utterly amazed with the speed that the ball moved up and down the field – by virtue of very athletic women, who possessed great stick skills, ran with gazelle-like speed and made assembly line passes thrown with the incredible accuracy.

Prior to the mid-1990's the women's game was filled with a lot of enthusiasts, however, the general public was not widely aware of it. Erin Brown Millon, former University of Maryland standout, multiple year U.S. women's player, and former Women's Division director at US Lacrosse says, "There were still some basic opinions out there like – 'What is this game? What are they doing? It's not men's lacrosse. They have to stop on every whistle and people made fun about the bubble around players.' We just had to deal with that kind of mentality and a certain level of ignorance."

In fact, Erin had the challenge and opportunity to be very active in the transition from the game of old to the new awakening. After playing in the pre-Cindy Timchal dynasty days at Maryland and becoming a member of the U.S. women's team, she also went to work for a lacrosse equipment manufacturer. By assisting in the marketing for the company and promotion of the women's game through special events, she was able to get the ear of her bosses, "Hey, look, there's a market. Granted there isn't a lot of equipment, but nobody really has the market right now. There is something here." And there certainly was. Being an all-American and a U.S. women's national team member, the name recognition added some validity to the company and their intended focus on the women's game.

The women's game, however, was still very tempered because the leaders in women's lacrosse had at that point such a very strong hold on it and were very hesitant to any type of changes. There was great skepticism and concern that control of the women's game was going to be taken out of women's control. A major concern was that people wanted to change the women's game to make it more like the men's game, because the men's game was getting on TV and at times having coverage in periodicals and things that the women's game never ever got – pre 1996 Atlantic Olympics, the women's soccer team and volleyball and softball teams did all this incredible great stuff. So, there was a lot of skepticism about some of the new advances. That was quite an interesting time.

A pivotal point for the game of women's lacrosse was the merging of the United States Women's Lacrosse Association, the existing national governing body for over 60 plus years, with the men's game, to form US Lacrosse. The USWLA, in its 67 years of existence, took its responsibility very seriously. They did everything. They were focused on grass roots and fielding a national team, and focused on the rules of the game – they were writing the rules of the game which the Women's Division of US Lacrosse is still doing. It was pretty enormous in terms of the responsibility for the sport with a "bake sale" mentality, which educators and coaches were doing. Millon says, as she looks back on her career: "I had resigned from US Lacrosse to spend my time with my family. I couldn't have imagined a greater time for me to have been involved with and really sort of committing my life to the game, because that was such a critical thing to have a new unified governing body begin and to get started off on the right foot, and have all the correct "players" be involved and pave the new way for the "advanced" culture. It was really a great thing and all along during this whole time frame what was happening was seeing the women's collegiate game getting a lot more press."

Millon mentions two important areas in the re-evolution. The first shift occurred over the seven consecutive national championships coached by Cindy Timchal at the University of Maryland. This was, and still is, quite newsworthy and some tremendous players were coming out of the program at that time and they were getting some ink. All of a sudden the women's game was starting to blossom as people were turning their interest to it.

Millon says, "Cindy Timchal, in general, is a huge proponent of equal athletic rights for the women and when she came to Maryland, she put a lot of demands upon the athletic department to give her girls the same things that were being given to many of the other male teams. She was one of the most prominent people."

The second change was the involvement of Gary Gait, one of the greatest male players in the game, as an assistant coach with Maryland's women's team.

The Gait-Keeper of the Women's Lacrosse Re-Evolution

Gary's input began to change the face of how the women's game was played. He brought some unique concepts into the game as far as different stick skills to try. It was important that Gary had an appreciation for the women's game, and when he would go out and teach these girls these crazy new stick skills, he would do it while using a women's stick – which certainly shows a respect for the skill needing to be learned within the parameters of what you had to work with within the women's game. The game was changing as the new governing body was changing. Initially there were some reservations about Gary being involved in the women's game. If you know Gary, he is such a likable guy and good hearted and he really was going about this in the right way. He very quickly won over a lot of the skeptics and interestingly enough, shortly after he became the assistant coach, he was speaking to college coaches, doing clinics and was asked to comment on a variety of different things. Shortly after that many of the other top five, top ten teams started to change the way they were playing. It was really a neat thing to see.

— Erin Brown Millon, Former University of Maryland Standout and Former Women's Division Director at US Lacrosse

Millon says that "Women have always had this fear that the game was going to be taken away and changed into something that was, in layman's terms, sexier, or just towards what they were used to be seeing in the men's game."

Rules and Boundaries

Susie Ganzenmuller says, "People have always touted the women's game as having remained more true to the game the American/Canadian Indians first played – a fast, free flowing game played with minimal equipment and without hard, defined boundaries. When she first started officiating, natural landmarks were used, those that might pose a danger to players, such as trees, hedges, hills, fences, team benches, or a ditch, to define the playing field boundaries. Large natural grass playing fields were more available and not necessarily rectangular. The player nearest to the ball with her stick/feet when the ball crossed an imaginary line 4m away/inside from the hazard would be given possession of the ball to resume play.

With the increased number of multi-purpose fields that were contained by tracks, the boundaries in the US women's game gradually become more definite. In 2002 the international women's game experimented with hard boundaries, and in 2003 hard boundaries were voted in to the IFWLA rules. The international ball out-of-bounds rule is essentially the same as the rule in men's lacrosse. Hard boundaries have made the international women's game more spectator friendly. They reward good defense, encourage more accurate passing/catching near the boundary, and the out-of-bounds/change of possession decisions by the officials are more consistent. The US Lacrosse Womens' Division Rules Committee voted in hard boundaries, effective 2006.

Another recent change in the women's game has been the addition of a restraining line drawn across the full width of the field, 27m from the goal line. In the 1990's the women's game became more of a running game and less of a passing game. If a team had possession of the ball, their entire team was on offense; the team without the ball was on defense. It was not unusual to see, 10 or 11 defense and the same number of attack, within 15m of goal. The midfield was lost, and all of the players packed in front of goal made it very difficult for players to find the space to cut, complete passes and shoot safely. The umpires also had difficulty managing play around the goal to keep the game safe and fair. The offside rule has solved the problems it was designed to address; it has opened up the space in front of goal and the midfield fast break passes have returned to the game. Most all new rules are designed to make the game more safe and to keep it flowing.

For all the years that she has been officiating, Susie claims that, "Women have been passionate about our game being a traditionally and comparatively safe sport to play without mandating additional protective equipment. In recent years women have become physically stronger, they are equally skilled with the crosse in their right or left hand, and crosse design has evolved from the traditional planar wooden crosse to the lighter, more flexible and minimally offset plastic molded head crosse." These changes now allow women to throw and shoot the ball with greater accuracy and speed. While the women's rules have always been based on safety first and have allowed players to wear some protective equipment, liability concerns have increased in every aspect of life in the USA. Since the 1980s, mouth guards are mandatory, not only to protect players' teeth but to limit the effects of head concussion. Goalkeepers are required to wear helmets with face guards, throat protectors, and chest protectors. Goalkeeping gloves and leg pads are also mandatory at the grassroots level of the game but remain optional for the higher levels of play. Until January 2005, thin gloves, eye protection and soft helmets were optional equipment for field players; however, eye protection now is required at all levels of play to prevent the rare but catastrophic occurrence of eye injury.

Ganzemuller believes that the jury is still out whether or not mandating eye protection will make the game safer or encourage players to risk attempting more dangerous checks around an opponent's head. She remembers, "I lived in Connecticut in the late 1980s when helmets were mandated for high school women's lacrosse play in Massachusetts. The game was more physical, and I remember a Massachusetts high school graduate telling her new collegiate lacrosse coach, 'This game is so quiet without a helmet.'" Massachusetts no longer requires high school girls' players to wear helmets.

This book asks important questions of well-meaning and well-intentioned lacrosse participants. The following question, and others in this book, will help the reader reflect about what matters most.

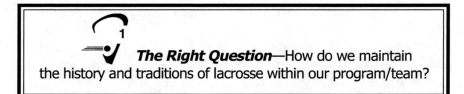

The Right Question—How do we maintain the history and traditions of lacrosse within our program/team?

Chapter 2

The Game and the People

*On the last night of the lacrosse camps I direct every summer, I testify
to some ideas that have over time become quite dear to me.
Right now, I say to the boys, as we sit here, the field we play
on is dark, empty space. It derives its meaning and value
solely from our presence. What we do while in that space
defines it, which is why we must do our best to author upon it
our very best selves. Those who will follow us to this field,
even long after we have left it, will know us by what we have
done here—if not personally, then intuitively and energeti-
cally. In the same way, if we approach the game with lucidity
and stillness, we can celebrate and draw upon the spirit of
those who have preceded us in playing it. This is the invisible
history of the game, and it stretches back over many years.
We owe them, past and future, as we owe ourselves, our best
effort.*

> —Kevin Hicks, Former Assistant Women's Coach at
> Brown University, Current Dean of Berkeley College
> at Yale University

The Stories of the Game and the People

When we demonstrate our "best effort" as a coach,
player, administrator, official or parent/spectator we also become
fully part of the game and have the greatest opportunity to enjoy
the process. As human beings, however, we have many aspira-
tions, motives and desires that drive our participation in lacrosse
on the field, sidelines or in the stands. This motivation can't be
totally deciphered or illustrated from a brief bio sketch in the team
program, blowing the whistle or cheering from the third row.

I have taken license to relate to lacrosse what Mark Waymack, who wrote an article about the importance of narrative and medical ethics, says, "If, however, we can 'learn' the (players) story, we learn what drives the biography. The things of greatest importance to the (player), his or her hopes, fears, and ambitions, are within the story. And as we hear the preceding chapters, it begins to discern how the next chapter should be written." Although there seems to be a greater desire for coaches to be able to make strategies and techniques brief and concise, the rituals of the game cannot be adequately discussed in a short blip, sound byte or bullet point. These enduring characteristics are best observed and discussed from the experience of the narrative, the stories that make up the lacrosse experience. This understanding comes from our own experience and the experience of others and can be best learned in a deeper, meaningful story-telling form.

The rich stories of the game that have accompanied our lacrosse experiences have certainly inspired belief and a sense of purpose within us. As we listen to the stories of our players, it is essential to listen for the cues that uncover their beliefs and sense of purpose. By doing so, we are more able to empathize with their joys, elations, frustrations and troubles.

Competition and Collaboration

Lacrosse is made better when competition and collaboration are appropriately balanced. Competition, in and of itself, is generally a very healthy process. There continues to be debate on whether competition is an instinctual or learned process. Perhaps it is a combination of both. However, when the whistle blows – and this team and that team meet – there is also a collaborative experience. And all the actors are now on the stage - an integration of teams, coaches, parent/spectators and officials. Competition and collaboration merge as all "step over the line" to participate in the dance. The collaborative experience is best observed when all participants genuinely care about the game – an unconditional positive regard for everyone involved being provided with the opportunity to have a great experience. This is also seen in a close match where each team pushes the other to perform well.

When I moved from Boston to The Culver Academies, I inherited a team of good athletes with good lacrosse skills. From the grandstand, it certainly appeared that we did well – scored a lot of goals, made lots of saves, won lots of games. It took the next three years, however, of continually re-addressing the importance of "connection" and respect for the game to be established. When the sense of connection finally crystallized with team members, we continued to perform well and also enjoyed the game much more. The players realized that respect for the game and others really mattered. This process – how we went about doing business on and off the field – was essential to satisfaction and enjoyment. This freed up our team to experience a sense of "completeness" much more often, and in turn improve individual and team performance.

Drew Hyland, a notable sports philosopher, once said that the goal of sport is to attempt to feel a sense of "completeness". When players, coaches, officials, and parents are involved in positive lacrosse experiences where "all the planets are aligned," there is a joyful, complete feeling. However, the nature of lacrosse, as any other sport, challenges all of us every time we "step on to the field or enter the stadium" – a sacred space that invites us to experience joy, happiness, frustration and satisfaction. They are all part of the human condition.

Loss and Rebirth

Lacrosse players have a finite or limited time in their lifetime to play the game. Whether one picks up a stick in childhood, or is seen loping down the field in a grandmaster's game, the experience can be very fulfilling. When the playing days end for many, they vicariously live out their love of the game through either coaching or introducing their sons or daughters to the game. Every time there is change, there can be a rebirth to another experience.

The research is clear that when two teams play, there will be a winner, a loser and an occasional tie game – a by-product of the competitive experience. However, the experience of winning and the experience of losing inevitably teach us something about ourselves – individually and as a team. It is quite amazing to fondly remember a great experience on the field and have that transfer to future performance. At the same time, how we learn from a previous sub-par performance and come back to play very well in another game can be very instructive. Every experience we have in life – every moment – we cannot recover. While we cannot change past experiences, we do have the ability to change how we think and feel about these experiences and thus learn to act appropriately when similar situations arise. Lacrosse is merely the vehicle to compartmentalize these emotions – to take loss and turn it into a rebirth.

A great high profile example of loss and rebirth happened during the 2005 NCAA Men's Division I semifinal game between Johns Hopkins University and the University of Virginia. The game saw a variety of momentum shifts on the field–so typical of lacrosse. When UVA scored with time running out in the final period, the Cavalier bench erupted and thousands of blue and orange clad fans went "Wahoo". However, as the great radio icon Paul Harvey says, "And now the rest of the story." Hopkins comes down off the face-off and scores with one second left on the clock to force overtime and eventually win the game. From the heights of excitement, to the depths of disappointment, lacrosse provides us with a whole constellation of emotions that help us in our shared identity with each other, the other team, coaches, and parents and fans.

Around the same time Virginia was playing Hopkins in that NCAA tournament game, the Culver team was playing in a consolation game following our 8-5 loss in the Indiana High School Lacrosse Association semifinals the night before. This sense of loss for participants of both UVA and Culver goes beyond the final score. It was a bittersweet ending for the graduating seniors at UVA, but they still carry on the "Hoo" identity into other life ventures. Although Indiana lacrosse is a far cry from Division I ball, two seniors on our team who weren't the best of friends, were very affected by our semifinal loss in the state tournament.

During the final week of school after the season, I observed them spending more time together connecting in their "shared identity." Although they would have liked to have seen a more favorable outcome during the playoffs, their emerging friendship was delightfully unexpected.

Alice Von Hildebrand cites from one of Gabriel Marcel's plays: "'Your death is my death.' It is true when we lose someone we love, something dies within us. And this is both painful and fearful." This can also be said about losing lacrosse games and the change that happens to every team's membership every year. "However, as the sorrow abates, we may recognize that the inverse must also be true, that your life is my life." In most cases, we are "reborn" to play another day. Loss can come in the completion of an "undefeated" season; the graduation of team members; moving up to the U13's after having a great experience with fellow players and the coach at the U11 level.

I witnessed a memorable rebirth when I spoke with the 1999 UMass men's team after the loss of Eric Soparcasa (briefly mentioned in Chapter 1). Eric's untimely death prematurely ended the season for the team. UMass' last game of the season against Brown was cancelled due to the visitation and funeral services for Eric back in Long Island. Both teams had lackluster seasons. However, the loss of Eric also created several other losses. One being that the team didn't have closure for the end of the season – especially for the seniors. A mental health counselor who was working with the team from UMass health services suggested to the coaching staff that some sort of closure activity might be helpful for the players and coaches. They decided upon having an intrasquad maroon vs white scrimmage (which also included the coaches as well as the players). After I spoke to the team about the difficulties of loss and had some individual chats with several players who were hurting pretty bad, I followed the maroon and white groups on to Garber Field. The game reminded me of the movie *Sandlot*, a group of neighborhood boys gather at the local sandlot to play pick up baseball, and everybody was having a lot of fun. Everything was pure lacrosse. The enjoyment and elation of having an opportunity to be back on the field once again was contagious for players and coaches. Laughter, enthusiasm abounded amidst the near empty stadium that would have been embraced by vocal fans on a regular game day. Certainly the game didn't take away any of the players grief for their fallen team member. However, what the experience provided was a type of "rebirth" and the development of a "shared identity" for the remaining team members. I think of a testimonial that Kevin Hicks, former assistant coach for the women's program at Brown and now dean of Berkeley College at Yale, spoke at a memorial service for a Brown women's player who had passed away: "Hemingway said it best in *A Farewell to Arms*: 'The world breaks everyone then some become strong at the broken places.'" When we experience great disappointment in loss, we also have the opportunity to unite and help each other to become stronger at this one broken place – and this can happen through our shared identity.

The Red Queen Effect

Skeptics may disagree, but there is (or should be) a shared identity with teammates and opponents. The competitive experience can be enhanced when one understands that each person (including the opponent) is a part of the same game. My college philosophy instructor once told me that it is important to congratulate the opponent who pushed you to play well. Unfortunately, as the game grows, we continue to observe an "us against them" mentality. This has been noted in greater instances across the board from youth through college lacrosse. When this happens, the other team is treated as unfeeling objects rather than functioning human beings. John Corlett, of the University of Windsor, paints a compelling illustration about the growth of sports in a presentation entitled, "The Red Queen Effect: Avoiding Life's Treadmill." Corlett quotes the character of the Red Queen in Lewis Carroll's *Through the Looking Glass*.

The Red Queen says to Alice that, "It takes all the running you can do to keep in the same place. If you want to get somewhere else, you must run at least twice as fast as that!" This may sound familiar to lacrosse coaches today, and Corlett draws an important parallel from what the Red Queen says. He claims that:

> *In biology, the evolution of relationships that evolve between predators and their prey has been known as the Red Queen effect.Any adaptation in a prey species is matched in subsequent generations by counter-adaptations in predator species. As the hunted become faster and more agile, so are those that hunt them. This arms race escalates in perpetuity, with neither side ever able to gain sufficient advantage to be safe from the threat of being eaten or starved to extinction. Athletes are used to the Red Queen effect.They train to become stronger, faster, and more skilled, knowing that other athletes are doing the same. Their coaches devise new strategies, knowing that other coaches will find ways to render them obsolete. Most athletes end their careers knowing that they were defeated at least as many times as they were victorious, a clear indication of the Red Queen effect dictaing the nature of the competitive culture.*

Corlett claims that in living in this type of culture, it is nearly impossible to get ahead. Lacrosse is no exception. In the new millennium, stick technology allows for greater stick control and protective equipment is more light weight allowing for player maneuverability. Players are, for the most part, in better physiological condition. Like an Eveready battery, they can run faster and longer. Coaches at the high school and collegiate levels counter opponent's offensive and defensive packages, and/or just "simply" go back to the mechanics of sound fundamentals – stick work done with such deliberate rehearsal that the movement is second nature and mechanical. The Red Queen Effect is also very present in our youth, starting with their first stick, pads, and ball.

There is nothing inherently wrong with living out the Red Queen effect. Many players, coaches, officials, and parents do this all the time – and at all levels of the game. Living in an out-come/performance based world all of the time welcomes frequent frustration and a continuous struggle to find completeness. There-fore it is essential to look at the process—how do we receive enjoyment and satisfaction along the journey?

What changes is the helmets, styles of uniform, size, speed and skill of the players, but what endures and connects us are not only the history and traditions of the sport, but also the human relationships which are more difficult to quantify than shots on goal and ground balls picked up. What should not change is honoring the game and opponent by playing very hard at every opportunity and reveling in the opportunity to compete with a like-minded competitor. This is a value and behavior that endures and draws us back to the game every spring.

A Life Span Approach to Lacrosse

The development and formation of lacrosse players does not happen by accident. Our interests and motivations for our involvement in the game can be better understood from looking at our own history of lacrosse and/or other sport experiences. A life-span approach to the game can be best viewed from our earlier "movement" experiences. Truly, the young child is the "parent" of the future lacrosse player.

A Life Span Approach to Lacrosse

Informal Structure
Freedom of Movement
Challenge/Exploration

The Formal Structure
Purity of Experience
Contamination of Experience

Integration of Experience

The Informal Structure of Lacrosse

Generally, we first experience freedom of movement as infants. We are not restrained in our actions, and we are encouraged to respond instinctively to our surroundings. Some modern psychologists, most specifically Mihaly (Mike) Csikszentmihalyi, might suggest that the total freedom of a baby's movements produces a "flow" state, a concept associated with the extraordinary performances of good athletes. "Flow," described simply, is the feeling of control and confidence one has when the challenge of the task is matched by the skill to handle that challenge. In the state of original freedom, the newborn moves naturally and easily. See Chapter 6 for more information on "flow."

When a person first picks up a stick, there is a certain awkwardness associated with the mechanical extension of the body. Just as a young child begins to explore his or her surroundings, there is a freedom of movement that seems to naturally come when a person picks up their first lacrosse stick. As Missy Foote says, the "freedom of lacrosse also makes it special - the ability to run with your head up (no ball on the ground) makes it feel unbridled and joyful."

Challenge and exploration make up the second stage of the overall experience. Challenge is self-imposed at first and is related to one's own development. Moving intentionally through space is done with an emerging sense of control, and understanding of capabilities, as well as limitations. For example, a young child first rolls down a hill with a straight body. Next, the child rolls him or herself up into a ball and realizes that the travel down the slope is much faster. Not only is this the child's first Newtonian physics lesson, he or she acts the movement out for the sheer joy of it. This is related to lacrosse in ways that players test out different ways to best throw and catch the ball. I find great joy in watching novice boys try to shoot the ball sidearm. After counseling them on the effectiveness and efficiency of shooting the ball overhand at this time in their careers, I observe the ball being released too early, heading directly where it was aimed – the cone on the south corner of the end line. When the ball is released too late, it hits the unsuspecting left side attack man in the helmet.

And when released just right, the ball makes a nice path right into the awaiting goalies stick. This is the stuff that helps players discover what works and doesn't work. When I work with aspiring boys' and girls' goalies who refuse to change their inefficient starting position or don't step to the ball, I reply that it is important to stop the ball as effectively as possible – an action they are doing quite infrequently. For years, my inability to create change in their approach was finally relieved, when they individually viewed video tape of their biomechanics in the cage. The camera doesn't lie. Maybe I represented the parent who tells his or her children that they must do something a certain way or the highway, and the goalies were merely acting out their adolescent requirements, and had to do it on their own. Whatever works, works!

The Formal Structure of Lacrosse

When a child or adolescent first begins to play in a structured program, new tasks and challenges are provided for the new player. The adults, who serve as coaches, have the opportunity to help the player retain the internally motivated play while encouraging skill building and constantly improving technical and tactical understanding of the game. New players begin to understand the "right" and "wrong" ways to throw and catch, pick up ground balls, etc. Coaches have a very important responsibility at this time. This varies from the "command-control" coaching style, in which the coach drives all learning or the "conductor-composer" approach – the coach is "hands-off" allowing for the players to be creative and drive their own actions. We will address these styles in greater depth in Chapter 4.

Integration – Pay it Forward

Our experiences as young people eventually influence our responses as adults. As youth, high school, collegiate or post collegiate players, we transfer our experiences to those we eventually parent or coach. One coach I know, who had the best intentions for trying to provide the players with great experiences, seemed to miss the boat with the players. He remarked that his overly "hard charging" style was learned from his experience as a player under several of his coaches. "This is what I know about the game and what I bring to it. I don't know any other way to coach."

The integration stage can be really characterized as "giving back to the game." This act is akin to the more recent cliché "pay it forward." Authored by Catherine Ryan Hyde, *Pay It Forward*, is a book, a major motion picture, and a foundation (accessible on the web), that revolves around the altruistic actions of a young boy who does a school project. He does something "real good" for several people, and when they ask how they can pay him back, he tells them to "pay it forward" to several other people. The pyramid widens with acts of kindness. Giving back to the game or paying it forward as coaches, good teammates, helpful parents, and good officiating makes the game better overall. Hyde says that the *Pay it Forward* website "brings together, in one place, as many real stories as we can." Lacrosse participants have their real stories, many of which resonate to others the reason we are involved in such a great game.

Dee Stephan, the Connecticut chapter president and her husband, volunteer to run the local youth programs (having grown from one team per town to multiple teams for five area towns). "Our four children see us, as helping others, enjoying the outdoors, being active and enjoying a sport for the pure pleasure of playing the game... no monetary rewards, no accolades just enjoying our time with local kids and people, sharing something we love. The benefits of participation besides the obvious fitness level it takes to play is the fact that no matter how late you start playing you can impact your high school team, the learning curve is quick. Participation on a lacrosse team puts you into a unique fraternity that no other sport has. A total team effort teaches you so much about life."

The Participants

It is essential to examine the responsibilities and opportunities that adult mentors have in the education and development of the players in their charge. In what ways can coaches, athletic administrators, parents, officials and the Lacrosse industry identify and support those core virtues that are available through the joyful experience of sport? The formation of good character, like the acquisition of lacrosse skill, requires a solid work ethic, perseverance, and self-discipline, as well as respect for self, opponents, and teammates. These traits are the by-products of well-intentioned players working with self-confident and appropriately reflective adults who have challenged themselves to reach their full potential as mentors.

Lacrosse Participant Groups

All are Stakeholders in the Pursuit of Excellence

Coaches, players, administrators, parents/spectators, officials, the Lacrosse Industry and the National Governing Body (US Lacrosse) are the stakeholders in maintaining lacrosse participation as a meaningful and positive experience. The collaborative effort of all the stakeholders provides an opportunity for the joy of movement in a social setting that allows players to grow. When each stakeholder group declares the core values of lacrosse, the possibility of reaping the benefits of participation is enhanced. The whole is greater than the sum of its parts: When all participants involved in the game make an informed and conscious effort to bring the core values to action on the field, there is the greatest opportunity for enjoyment, satisfaction and enhanced performance.

Coaches at all levels have responsibilities as mentors, modelers and managers of their players. The field is the coaches' classroom as they aspire to create meaningful and worthwhile environments for their players based on developmentally appropriate strategies.

Players at the youth, high school, college and post-collegiate level have an opportunity to realize great joy and satisfaction from playing the game by embracing the core values of lacrosse.

Administrators, such as youth program coordinators, high school and college athletic directors, and club/elite team directors have a major responsibility in the compliance of core values and oversight in their respective lacrosse programs.

continued on next page....

> ....continued from previous page
>
> **Parents/Spectators** - Parents are the major educators of their children and by supporting the core values of lacrosse can provide a wonderful opportunity for their children. Spectators who demonstrate the core values in action while attending practices and games help to support the best possible experience for all participants.
>
> **Officials,** in their judicial responsibility make fair calls, and their reinforcement of proper conduct facilitates the best possible experience for the players. They ought to be viewed as working in partnership, in a collaborative effort with coaches.
>
> **The Industry** is represented by the various organizations and companies that provide other lacrosse stakeholders with products and services that are in accordance with and consideration of rules, safety and quality.
>
> **US Lacrosse Campaign for Excellence, March 2005**

Although it is 30 years ago this past April when it happened, I will always remember a brief interaction between one of my fellow college teammates and the opposing coach. Rob Pfeifer, then the Middlebury College men's coach, remembers calling time out in the middle of the game: "It was a hot day, and I wanted to give the players a breather. Suddenly, I felt the thud of a Boston State player jumping on my back from behind, yelling Lt. Pfeiffer, Lt. Pfeiffer! My players are all running towards me to defend their coach. There was this big hush and time stood still for a moment. I think we all were a bit befuddled." Evidently, Coach Pfeiffer's voice had registered with Ronny Ingemi, one of our midfielders. Ronnie had been playing lacrosse for a couple years since his return from Vietnam. To Ronnie, Pfeiffer's voice was clear as day, as he heard it in the rice paddies of Vietnam. This unexpected reunion still resonates in the minds of many of the Middlebury and Boston State players who were present that day and occasionally it is mentioned when they meet up each summer at the Vail Tournament.

John Pirani once mentioned that there are several adults that have the overall responsibility for a lacrosse game – the coaches, the officials and the attending administrator (not always attending, unfortunately). The adult stakeholders truly "drive the bus" regarding the flow and behavior of the game. Some will argue that the coach-official relationship is adversarial. And we know when this happens, more often than not, there are two competitions going on in the same game – one team versus the other team, and both teams versus the officials. When this happens, it invites "distraction" from providing the best experience for all participants. Of course, some novice officials may inadvertently dictate the flow of the game, while some over zealous coaches may exhibit their lack of effort in preparing their team for the game, by scapegoating the officials. These scenarios are not either-or events. It is important to understand that the game is primarily for the players – an assumption that not all coaches and officials totally buy into (which is unfortunate).

The game is made better when officials exhibit patience with players and coaches, especially with youth participants, while being instructive with youth and high school players. Good officials demonstrate a mastery of knowledge of the rules while embracing a healthy collaborative effort with coaches to ensure an appropriate experience for the players.

As an assistant coach with the Holy Cross College men's team in the early 1990's, I vividly remember the game in which I took it upon myself to ensure that the officials did the right thing on the field. I am not sure where this arrogance on my part came from. I had never said "boo" to an official in my playing and coaching career. It couldn't have my being an exuberant youth – I was 37 years old then. So, each time the official on the bench sideline ran by I would "work him." Third time down the sideline was a charm, but for an unexpected outcome – he stopped and looked directly into my eyes – it was only a second or two, but felt like an eternity – he told me to be quiet and do my job as a coach. He didn't flag me, but our brief interaction caused me to pause on my responsibility, not only as a coach, but as a stakeholder in the game. In another instance, some fellow teachers had never seen a game until a weekend of wonderful lacrosse during the 2004 Men's Championship Weekend. They mentioned that they were quite befuddled after watching the semi-finals on Saturday and the amount of "lip service" handed out to the officials that were not reciprocated with flags. At this level, lacrosse participants are visible ambassadors of the game and the game is much bigger than the two team competing. In this case, there were 40,000 spectators in person and many more watching on television.

We are all human. Officials make mistakes and coaches err. However, one lacrosse participant said it perfectly: "For an unprepared coach to try and make an official responsible for the coach's ignorance is a slight to the game." The opposite is also true – an unprepared official does not do justice to the game. The need for qualified coaches and officials starting at the youth level with both the men's and women's game is great. This issue can be likened to the growth of muscles, tendons and ligaments. Tendons and ligament do not grow as fast at muscle tissue does. With more muscle – players and team, we need a greater number of coaches (tendons) and officials (ligaments).

The US Lacrosse survey claims that 96 percent of the sample strongly agreed or agreed that coaches and officials have equal responsibilities in governing the overall behavior of the participants in a game.

Survey of Lacrosse Stakeholders

Coaches and officials have equal responsibilities in governing the overall behavior of the participants in a game.

		Number of Responses	Response Ratio
Strongly Agree	▬▬▬▬▬▬	*1047*	*66%*
Agree	▬▬▬	*469*	*30%*
Disagree	▪	*60*	*4%*
Strongly Disagree		*6*	*0%*
	Total	*1582*	*100%*

When parents and other spectators understand and reinforce the basic foundations of lacrosse tradition/culture to players, there is less distraction and the game is made better. A great example is the story that Eric Leimsieder, a former player at Indiana University, made public at a gathering of friends and family after the funeral of one of his fellow teammate's father.

We Are All Team

At the Indiana University Men's Club Lacrosse team's fall banquet during parent's weekend, O'Neal Turner (father of O'Neal III, a midfielder on the team) stood up to say a few words to the crowd. Prior to his ascension, the coach, assistant coach and captains spoke about the team. His brief recitation was unexpected and many in the audience were taken off guard. There was a silence when he began to speak. He shared with the parents that, "IU lacrosse was not only for the players, it was also for the parents. It was all about becoming one big family. When the players feel that they have our support, it makes them feel like they accomplish any task, beat any opponent."

— Eric Leimsieder, Indiana University Lacrosse '04

On the flip side, I once asked John Pirani about what happens when overzealous parents "butt in" during the game. He claims that parents aren't responsible for the contest. They are guests who have a wonderful opportunity to watch their children play. He speaks to the parents collectively prior to each season. He says, "I want you to be comfortable. I want your child to be comfortable. There shouldn't be a compelling reason to directly interact with your child during the game, so you don't need to stand on my sideline. Just watch the game and talk about it with your child over dinner." There is a compelling reason to empower parents to do what is right for their children. As an aside, John's teams won the 2000 and 2001 Massachusetts state championships. He didn't adjust his stance on coach and parent responsibilities during those two seasons nor any other season. His consistency of management has been crystal clear to his athletes and other stakeholders in the community for years.

Several years ago at Culver, we were playing an early Saturday morning home game against a rival team. Throughout the game the parents and other fans supporting the away team were becoming quite vocal in their feedback over the officials' calls. I sensed this behavior was becoming quite a distraction, not only to me, but also to both teams out on the field. I called a time out and asked the opposing coach if it would be okay for me to express to the parents that their behavior was unacceptable. They looked at me in shock when I dared tell them that "we do not do that here at our school." To compound the matter, one of my players took the liberty to rub my words in a little bit deeper by sharing his thoughts with the parents after I left. This, of course, created an uproar – that I wasn't aware of until after the game when the assistant coach of the other team informed me of my player's inappropriate behavior. Then several parents of that team came over and let me have it. Above all, I stood my ground on what I said to them and apologized for my player's action and let them know that I would take swift action to resolve my player's involvement, which I immediately did. This was a prime example of individual needs getting in the way of the whole process. Parents want their children to succeed and be safe when they play. Above all, there ought to be standards with teeth that remind us that we should appreciate that lacrosse is special and without entitlement, other than the sense of enjoyment that comes from goodwill, respect, being positive and honoring the game.

The Benefits and Opportunities of Lacrosse Participation

Every sport has its zealous advocates, those who would speak well of its virtues while perhaps not seeing its shortcomings. On the face of it, lacrosse is a sport that requires skill on an individual and team basis: a high level of cardiovascular conditioning; a sharp sense of competition. It offers a history that goes back hundreds of years. It's hard to argue with those virtues. In some ways, however, lacrosse requires a level of courage and teamwork that it seems few other sports do. Of course most sports offer many benefits, but as a field sport, lacrosse occupies a unique niche in most schools. It is the only spring sport that brings all of those benefits to the student-athlete.

Lacrosse participation offers benefits that are similar to participation in most sports: belonging to a team and working toward a common goal. Pat Dillon, chair of the US Lacrosse Board of Directors, sees camaraderie as one of the greatest benefits that the game offers. Alan McCoy has always believed that the common bond of playing together provides a special friendship, one that may never have developed among people without the shared goals of being on a team. The opportunities are learning about oneself through challenge and competition, while experiencing both success and failure. Dave Campbell, former All-American goalie at Middlebury College and now head men's coach at Connecticut College, says the biggest benefit of playing the game is the same as from playing any team sport. "The lessons you learn come from being a part of a team and having a bunch of individuals working towards a common goal. I think our sport is still played for the love of the game and is pure in that sense. They play because they love being a part of the game." Noel Ebner, a US Lacrosse Youth Council representative from Syracuse, sees lifelong value in the game. "When the people involved in lacrosse keep perspective, you can't get away from it!"

Development of the Whole Person

Sue Stahl, former head coach of the U.S. women's national team and coach at Old Dominion University, maintains that lacrosse teaches a woman to balance the physical, emotional and mental dimensions of the sport. It can be a bit more frustrating learning lacrosse than other sports, but a balanced approach to the game can provide great rewards. Erin Brown Millon played for Coach Stahl and has greatly benefited from her wisdom. Erin remarks that the people of lacrosse have made such a great difference in her life. "I had great respect for the women who came before, who did without—those who paved the way—that type of thing—but I also had the forward thinking of wanting women athletes to get their just desserts and for people to appreciate the women's game for what it was and not to see it as something to change. I was very attuned to wanting to see that kind of thing happen."

Self-Discipline, Confidence and Collaboration

Jim Wilson is considered the dean of independent school lacrosse in New England with almost 50 years of coaching (I played against the team he coached in a high school/prep all-star game in 1971). He sees lacrosse as a free flowing, great transition, that really depends on the ability of young athletes to make split-second decisions under pressure. "Taught properly, it can help kids be more self-reliant and independent . . . defense can be, and is, orchestrated to a large degree, but the beauty of the game comes in the transition and in unscripted offensive play – much like hockey at its best, but better because the athletes can control the ball and the flow better than they can control the puck," he says. He believes the benefits and opportunities depend mostly on how the coaches approach the sport... whether it is an opportunity for self expression and flow and creativity and decision-making under pressure – or whether it is scripted. The latter ruins the game, denying athletes wonderful opportunities. Gordon Webb agrees with Jim, "Lacrosse is fun! It is fun to play catch, it is fun to practice, and it is fun to play the game. It is a free flowing game where the individual player has the opportunity for self-expression within the structure and strategy of the team. Lacrosse also provides so many opportunities for great acquaintances and friendships." As with athletics in general, lacrosse provides an excellent environment for the development of positive behavioral characteristics such as perseverance, work ethic, loyalty, commitment, dependability, and integrity.

Jordy Almgren, former president of the Indiana High School Lacrosse Association, an official and current head boy's coach at Blessed Theodore Guerin High School in Indianapolis, remarks that the benefits that lacrosse provides are many, including the inclusion vs. exclusionary nature of some traditional sports. There is a unique ability to teach a player a contact sport that does not always call for physical play. The nature of this type of split second decision carries itself forward with players in real-life scenarios where decisions need to be measured and carried out in short order. This can be carried out at all different levels of the game. The mantra of "there is no such thing as an ex-lacrosse player" is more accurate now then ever before.

Connections and Friendships

Kate Dresher sees girls' youth lacrosse as being about friendships, about having fun while still challenging the players with a little bit of competition. Dee Stephan says, "No matter where I go, lacrosse coaches, fans, players and refs want to share their knowledge of the game with anyone who will ask and listen. Lacrosse people are not shy about calling up someone from another town or state and saying, 'I heard you need a game or I heard you have a great play for ...' It doesn't matter if it is some-one you might play or compete against, lacrosse people share their love of the game and their knowledge like no other sport does. The speed and grace of the game itself make the game special but it's truly the people that make lacrosse unique from other sports."

Steve Bristol, head men's coach at St. Mark's School in Southborough, MA, reflects on the popular credit card's tag line: "membership has its privileges." "The privileges are clearly the relationships you engender through connection with other lacrosse players," Steve says. "You share a common bond or connection that comes through participation in this unique game. This con-nection plays out in a similar way to attending a small college, and then meeting someone later in life who went to the same place. You have an immediate connection that takes the relationship to another level faster than it normally would go. That connection translates into business and job opportunities, friendships, etc."

Kristen Corrigan played her college ball at the University of Virginia and tended her craft for another ten years on the U.S. women's team. As the current head coach at Culver Girls Academy, she says the benefits of participation include the confidence and commitment to learn to deal with adversity; and the strong connections and relationships that carry past the lacrosse world.

Cross-Team Camaraderie

Last year, after our second game with Lexington, I worked my way up the handshake line at the end of the game. I noticed it was moving more slowly than those lines typically move and stepped out for a second to see what was going on up front. We play Lexington twice a year and as a neighboring community, the players are very familiar with one another. The reason the line was going slowly was the boys were chatting rather amiably, pausing with helmets in hand, exchanging a few words, waving to the moms and dads of the other team who were waiting a few yards to the side of the line. Other sports certainly share that kind of cross-team camaraderie, but seeing it in action and then mirroring the boy's behavior with my colleague who was at the end of his team's line exemplified the best in sportsmanship and an unpracticed team behavior that certainly speaks well of lacrosse. Similarly, I have gone through lines and had a rather large teen from the other team greet me warmly. His response to my befuddlement is usually disappointment, but when I engage the boy in a conversation, I usually find out we were in camp together three or four years ago. I guess that means I changed less than he did.

— John Pirani, Head Boy's Coach, Winchester High, MA

Dom Starsia believes that lacrosse has meant everything to him. "For me, it's been everything. I take the job home. I take my family to the office. There is no separation for me. There never has been. I've grown up in the game. I've been coaching at the collegiate level full-time for 31 years. I've been coaching longer than my athletes have been alive. There is such a sense of community in our game." Starsia remarks that the game is still small enough that, "We all know each other's business and so, if a kid acts like a jerk at a camp, it is really hard to shake that reputation in our sport. You carry that around with you for a long time. Sometimes the game seems a little too small, but it is still endearing." Shaun Stanton, head boy's coach at St. Sebastian's school says, "There is a community of lacrosse players that is very inclusive and a great deal of networking can be done with in this community."

Ricky Fried has gained a new perspective on lacrosse after coming into the women's game. He claims that it builds confidence, develops interpersonal skills within the players because they have to deal with each other. Ricky says, "It creates bonds that last a lifetime for most of them. Without a doubt they stay in touch with those same people regardless of where they end up after lacrosse. Because of the huge network it gives them opportunities to deal with other lacrosse people within the web of ties and connections outside of the college world and into the business world – pretty much whatever direction they want to go in."

"Officiating has allowed me to participate in a sport that I never played but loved from the first game I ever saw," says Susie Ganzenmuller. "It affords me the opportunity to be a positive role model for young people and my peers. I have high ethical standards; sportsmanship and fair play are important values to me in all aspects of my life. Officiating teaches integrity, courage, teamwork, responsibility, humility in honest self-evaluation, and it hones ones work ethic, decision-making and interpersonal skills. While I have good and bad days on the field, I LOVE officiating! I enjoy teaching others to officiate, and in doing so, my game improves, and hopefully I am able to pass on my passion for the game."

Brad Jorgenson, a member of the aforementioned "Springfield Mafia" and now coach at Wheaton College, says that, "Even the most well-funded programs have modest backgrounds and tend to be fiercely protective of the sport they love. The ability to "speak lacrosse" to another fan of the game seems to be more of a bonding experience for lacrosse players. This appreciation of the game, its history, and what the game has done for an individual is a topic that never gets boring. Most men that have played lacrosse still claim many of their best friendships came through lacrosse. The combination of team, history, and a sense of duty make both the individuals and groups involved in the game uniquely prepared for the world away from the field."

Lacrosse's Chain of Connection – Six Degrees of Separation

Six degrees of separation was a theory first proposed in 1929 that suggests that most people can be connected to other people through a succession of no more than five social contacts. Some may be familiar with the party game – Three Degrees of Kevin Bacon – based on how the actor can be linked to many of other actors based on their shared work in the movies. This chain is evident in lacrosse today. I was amazed at the connections I realized through the interview process for the book.

When I met Jordy Almgren in 2000, he told me he had played for Will Graham at Gould Academy in Maine. Will and I played against each other in college, Will at Middlebury and I at Boston State. In fact, we were both spectators to Ronnie Ingemi jumping on Will's coaches back in the middle of a game. Will and I later became fast friends when we both played for the Brine Club team back in the late 70's. Our connection to Jordy and coach Rob Pfeiffer has helped get Will and I back in touch with each other.

2

The Right Questions—How extensive are your lacrosse connections? How have they enabled you to flourish in the game? Who are the lacrosse people who have really made a difference? How do our associations with other lacrosse participants bring us enjoyment and satisfaction?

SECTION 2

The Continuing Education and Safety of All Participants

Chapter 3

The Purpose and Vision of the Game

They don't need just information; they need meaningful information. They don't need just knowledge; they need knowledge that makes sense and inspires belief. They need knowledge that helps them understand why learning and living are worthwhile.
—Kevin Ryan & James Cooper; *Those Who Can, Teach*

Strong leadership requires a commitment to providing quality guidance and instruction and a safe physical, emotional, mental, moral and social climate for all participants. When applied to lacrosse, this commitment results in a knowledgeable community and enables trust between participant groups. People at different ages and development levels do different things for different reasons. Playing lacrosse welcomes challenge and elation, enjoyment and disappointment – all parts of the human condition.

Just as stick skills, conditioning, and a sense of game flow are important technical aspects of lacrosse, they are typically achieved when there are established guidelines within the team/program. Specific goals, objectives, philosophy, and underlying principles are essential to the success of the teams. Its about taking care of the "big rocks" in the bag. US Lacrosse's vision extends to this end:

> *We envision a future that offers people everywhere the*
> *opportunity to discover, learn, participate in, enjoy,*
> *and ultimately embrace the shared passion of the*
> *lacrosse experience.*

In many ways, playing the game passionately, with commitment, invites a level of "intimacy," or closeness or shared identity with coaches and teammates. This shared identity typically emerges when, as sociologist Steve Glenn claims, all participants on a team or in a program: are listened to; are taken seriously; feel genuinely needed; and have a meaningful purpose.

The importance of proper goal-setting in lacrosse cannot be over emphasized. The fundamentals of the game revolve around the development of second-nature habits through on-going repetition. Improving skills, techniques and tactics through a structured "goal setting" system can enable the realities of improvement to be more satisfying and beneficial to the player and coach. Ninety-nine percent of the participants surveyed agreed or strongly agreed that it is important for teams/programs and coaches to clearly outline goals and objective that establish appropriate guidelines.

Survey of Lacrosse Stakeholders

It is important for teams/programs/coaches to clearly outline
goals and objectives that establish appropriate guidelines.

		Number of Responses	Response Ratio
Strongly Agree		*932*	*59%*
Agree		*629*	*40%*
Disagree		*13*	*1%*
Strongly Disagree		*1*	*0%*
	Total	*1575*	*100%*

Goal Setting

Lacrosse, in and of itself, is a purposeful activity, whether it be wall ball, a three-person drill, a scrimmage or a game. When done appropriately, the demonstration of attainable goals that measure improvement is essential to individual and team success at all levels of the game. A goal is an objective, standard or aim of some action. It is important to distinguish between subjective and objective goals, in that the goal setting is most effective when the lacrosse player establishes clear and consistent aims. Subjective goals are based on individual judgment or discretion, thereby making them difficult to measure. Often subjective goals are represented by such outcomes as "having fun" or "doing one's best."

SMART GOALS

The acronym **SMART** provides a useful tool for developing a goal-setting strategy.

S = **specific** goals – The coach and/or player clarifies what he or she is committed to achieving. The player who wants to increase his or her number of successful wall ball throws and catches in a certain period of time has a specific goal; the player who just want to "throw and catch better" does not. The clearer the goal, the better the chance the athlete will develop a strategy to achieve the goal. Coaches ought to set specific goals with their players so the players have a strong understanding of what "exactly" they need to achieve. The important question to ask is, "What is the specific skill, etc. to be achieved."

M = **measurable** goals – The previous example also illustrates measurability. Measuring "getting better" is a subjective process, whereas "increasing number of successful throws and catches" is objective. The important question to ask is, "How is the completion of the goal assessed and gauged?"

A = **adjustable** goals – Once a goal is set, particularly a long-term goal, the player must be willing to adjust what he or she originally committed to achieving. For example, the player may be slowed down by injury, over-training or some other factor as he or she comes closer to achieving the goal. The important question to ask is, "What are potential barriers and other variables that may inhibit a player or coach's realization of goal, and how can the goal be re-structured?"

continued on next page....

....continued from previous page

R = realistic goals - Setting goals that are too lofty invites disappointment. While aspiring and dreaming long into the future can be inspirational, it is important that the player and/or team be successful with short-term goals. The important question to ask is, "How is the goal practical or realistic – is it too easy or too difficult?"

T = time-sensitive goals - This process requires a commitment to declaring when the goal will be achieved. There is a distinct difference, for example, between a lacrosse player's statement that he or she will increase the accuracy of his or her shot by 10 percent, and the commitment to increasing on-cage accuracy by 10 percent at the end of a three-month period. Setting a time limit imposes a sense of urgency for the athlete to create an appropriate strategy with a realistic timeline. The important question to ask is, "What is the time-line for achieving the specific goal?"

Although these outcomes are desirable, it is more effective to establish objective and measurable goals, such as attaining a specific standard of proficiency on a task in a specified time period. Examples of objective goals for lacrosse players might include: increasing the number of throws and catches over a certain period of time in wall ball; proper execution during line drills or shuttles based on percentage of successful catches. Also, it is more effective to set personal and team performance goals rather than outcome based goals based on comparisons with other athletes.

The US Lacrosse survey indicated that a significantly higher percentage (84.5 percent) of girls' interscholastic and women's college participants believed that "learning to set goals" was a reason for participation in the game. Boys' high school and men's college interest was 75 percent.

Survey of Lacrosse Stakeholders

Learning to set goals is a reason for participation

	Agree/Strongly Agree
Girl's Interscholastic	*83%*
Women's College (D1,2,3)	*86%*
Boy's Interscholastic	*77%*
Men's College (D1,2,3)	*73%*

Having a clear purpose is essential, and should be understood and declared by all stakeholders. Although this ought to happen at every level of the game, I was moved by a keynote talk by Dom Starsia, the University of Virginia men's coach, at the 2004 US Lacrosse National Convention in Philadelphia. My major intent of attending the convention was to reconnect with the large network of high school coaches throughout the country, check-in with coaches to finalize the 2004 Indiana schedule, and attend some meaningful technical and strategy sections to look at different ways to present our X's and 0's for the 2004 season. However, what struck me most was Starsia's talk. I have known Dom since we first played together on the Brine Lacrosse Club team in the late 1970s. He is arguably one of the best coaches in Division I—a true "double-goal coach"—and he conveyed, through his talk and a pre-season letter he sent to his 2003 team, what really matters most to attain success in the Virginia program. His words and prose rang very clear to me and my fellow coaches that, in many ways, this is similar to many lacrosse programs, albeit at different skill levels. He talked about having "one goal" in mind for the whole team, since many games are decided by "one goal." Coach Starsia mentioned that he has typically been a "hands-off coach" with off-field behavior. However, he began to realize that it was indeed influencing the success of Virginia and then began to address it. The following is just a sampling of his letter:

One Goal

I have often said that the difference in play between two teams in a one-goal game is so disproportionate to how the two teams feel about themselves upon the game's conclusion. What is the difference in play between the two teams? Sixty minutes, or more, of lacrosse, all those groundballs, those individual battles, deflecting a pass, making a save, etc., and, one final shot determines the outcome.

The top programs attain (and maintain) their status because they believe in the philosophy of the program – style of play, standard of behavior on and off the field, respect for each other's practice environment, etc. In turn, a player on one of these top teams is already one of the very best college players in the country. So, how does someone at this level improve, how does a program at this level improve itself, how do you improve your chances of having the winning result in one of these close games? WORK HARDER!, sure – but there are a limited number of hours in the day and everyone "works hard" . . . WORK BETTER!, definitely, always modifying the lifts, adjusting practice, trying to improve the individual workouts, thinking of creative ways to improve our business. We spend most of our time with this one. What I am certain of is that as you move toward the top, greater effort is required for any improved results. This is not meant to discourage – the rewards at the top are also much more meaningful."

—Dom Starsia, UVA Lacrosse, December 2002

James Kouzes and Barry Posner in *The Leadership Challenge* state that leadership is "the art of mobilizing others to want to struggle for shared aspirations." Modern day leaders "don't command and control; they serve and support." Kouzes and Posner stress the importance of motivating people to "want to" work for shared goals. The authors believe that mandating followership is not nearly as effective as creating a vision of success, sharing that vision, and encouraging, rather than directing, people to embrace it. Today's coaches must realize that authority is only as important as the respect that attends it. Embracing this model will result in stronger leadership, more loyalty, and greater satisfaction for coaches and their players.

The Quality of the Lacrosse Experience

Meaningful events, brief encounters from a memorable play or valuable interactions with a teammate or opponent all represent a quality lacrosse experience. When we are purposeful in our approach to the game – whether it be a combination of fun and skill development, etc., then we fully become part of the event and more freed up to enjoy the process.

Some people remark how difficult it must be for good friends to coach against each other, whether it be in the NCAA championship or an Under 13 Youth game. The US Lacrosse survey indicates that 9 percent of the respondents either agree or strongly agree that the quality of a participant's lacrosse experience is just as important as the results of the performance. Of course, the degree of quality of the experience may be strongly related to the final score or other statistics. Participants' quality of lacrosse experience is reflected in how they master their craft and eventually the environment in which they perform. Ninety-two percent of the US Lacrosse survey respondents agree or strongly agree the quality of the lacrosse experience is just as important as the results of the performance. Further examination that supports the importance of a blended mastery and performance climate suggests a motive for their participation in the game is to create friendships (93 percent); win competitions (73 percent); learn new skills (90 percent); improve skills (94 percent) and have fun (99 percent). The US Lacrosse survey also indicates that lacrosse promotes self-improvement, general well-being, cooperation, enjoyment, team cohesion and skill development in 97-99 percent of respondents.

The Right Question – What are the things that lacrosse promotes in your life?

Survey of Lacrosse Stakeholders

In general, I participate in lacrosse to:

	Strongly Agree	Agree	Disagree	Strongly Disagree
Work on weaknesses	23%	42%	29%	6%
	321	581	407	84
Create friendships	41%	52%	7%	1%
	583	741	98	14
Win competitions	25%	48%	21%	5%
	353	678	299	77
Learn new skills	44%	46%	8%	2%
	624	650	108	27
Improve skills	52%	42%	4%	1%
	736	597	61	19
Have fun	76%	23%	1%	0%
	1099	331	10	2
Be a star	9%	20%	46%	26%
	120	274	631	358

A name that kept on coming up in my interviews regarding "quality of lacrosse experience" was Dick Garber. Garber was and still is a legend in New England lacrosse. He was probably one of the most respected men in the game for a variety of reasons, but most importantly, his ability to make any player or coach – his own or an opponent – feel as if he/she was the only person in the world when he spoke with you. When Greg Cannella, a former player for "Garbs", first got the head job at UMass, he asked Coach Garber for advice. "He told me: 'Don't lose focus of why you are in this... the kids!' For a coach those are words to live by! Translating purpose and vision is difficult when you are dealing with 17- to 22-year olds – many of them do not have vision past the next day! So I try to incorporate my personal experiences at that age and present day to talk about their possible futures and that of the team."

What a Wonderful World – Living Lacrosse Full Circle

The satisfaction and feeling of accomplishment for playing lacrosse (1967-1969) at the University of Massachusetts for Dick Garber, a true gentleman to all, instilled in me a sense of pride and purpose that has helped define my philosophy on life. He was a man of strength, character and humility. His influence left an imprint that will never be forgotten by me, the hundreds of players he coached or the countless people that were lucky enough to know him. Even in death he was still teaching, at his funeral mass service the music he told his family to play was "What a Wonderful World" by Louis Armstrong. What a wonderful man! My sense of purpose! I have been teaching and coaching lacrosse for over 30 years and started two varsity lacrosse programs in Billerica and North Andover Massachusetts, two youth lacrosse organizations, coached for six years at the University of Lowell, and four with the Boston Blazers in the NLL. What a blast, doing something you really enjoy. Everything has gone "full circle," my oldest son, Ryan played for UMass and graduated in the spring of 2005 and my other son, Jim, is now a freshman at UMass. Talk about tradition.

As for my players, I ask them: Why are you here? Why do you want to play? And sometimes I have to convince young athletes to try out for the team. They give different reasons for playing, but I believe they are looking for a purpose and I hope I can help them with their vision. I try to teach them the game of lacrosse, tell them a few stories, and help them to understand themselves and the value of competing in the great game of lacrosse.

—Steve Connolly, Head Boys' Coach, North Andover High School, MA

Establishing Core Values

During July 2004, US Lacrosse assembled stakeholders from all constituencies of the game to develop a "branding statement" for the national governing body. From that meeting, seven core concepts, or what can be called core values were expressed: connection, leadership, respect, tradition, spirit, trust and youth.

It seems that successful lacrosse programs are those that have a clear purpose and vision. Unfortunately, too few coaches and program administrators appreciate the need to write down what is absolutely clear to them. Could writing down a team's foundational beliefs, its ethos, actually result in better performance? Additionally, few important adult stakeholders see the important connections between their school's mission statement (if they have one) and what happens with their lacrosse teams. Finally, not all coaches or administrators see the need to involve participants in creating a set of commitments that go beyond training rules. What could these athletes possibly add to the dialogue that we (adults) have not considered or included? Consequently, ideas or views are shared informally, without commitment; and, often the subsequent actions of the team or its members are not indicative of what was collectively approved in the pre-season.

A business analogy can be helpful. Most businesses ask all employees to understand and sign a code of ethics. Imagine what can happen if managers are not successful in convincing their employees to declare their support for these documents. The idea of declaring a program's core values is not new. Many businesses now have made the use of guiding principles attractive when they unveil their credos as a way of evaluating any and all of the company's decisions. If the activity supported the credo, it was appropriate and reasonable. While this seems obvious, many programs have not taken the time to establish any agreements. The credo, which serves to identify and emphasize virtuous behavior, provides a foundation for expectations of behavior.

The 30-Second Commercial

A simplified activity that can help lacrosse programs – including players, coaches, administrators and parents - is the 30-Second Commercial. Ask players, coaches, parents and administrators of your lacrosse program the following question: "If your lacrosse team or program were to come up in conversation, internally or externally, what would you want others to say about it?" This question asks the participant to declare what he or she believes matters most in the lacrosse program. This exercise is called the 30-Second Commercial because it asks program stakeholders to advertise their lacrosse program in a brief, clear, and concise manner. Figure # 1 that follows presents the questions.

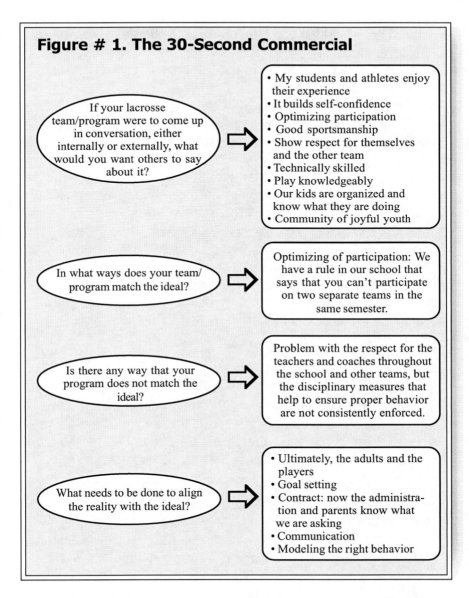

Figure # 1. The 30-Second Commercial

If your lacrosse team/program were to come up in conversation, either internally or externally, what would you want others to say about it?

⇨

- My students and athletes enjoy their experience
- It builds self-confidence
- Optimizing participation
- Good sportsmanship
- Show respect for themselves and the other team
- Technically skilled
- Play knowledgeably
- Our kids are organized and know what they are doing
- Community of joyful youth

In what ways does your team/program match the ideal?

⇨

Optimizing of participation: We have a rule in our school that says that you can't participate on two separate teams in the same semester.

Is there any way that your program does not match the ideal?

⇨

Problem with the respect for the teachers and coaches throughout the school and other teams, but the disciplinary measures that help to ensure proper behavior are not consistently enforced.

What needs to be done to align the reality with the ideal?

⇨

- Ultimately, the adults and the players
- Goal setting
- Contract: now the administration and parents know what we are asking
- Communication
- Modeling the right behavior

The second part of the exercise asks: "In what way does your program match the ideal?" In other words, are the stakeholders in the program doing what they want others to think they are doing? The third part asks: "Is there any way that your program doesn't match the ideal?" This question asks the stake-holder to analyze any areas that may need improvement. Finally, it asks: "What can you do to adjust the program so it can be in greater alignment?"

The value of the 30 Second Commercial is that it asks participants to "declare" themselves in sharing what they believe to be important for the lacrosse team or program. When there is consensus with the "commercial," this declaration of core vales can be used as a document that all participants abide by – in turn making the game better since all, or at least hopefully a majority of stakeholders, have bought into common purposes.

An example of a 30 Second Commercial may include traits such as: teaching life lessons; winning; instilling a love of the game; and honoring the game. The US Lacrosse survey asked respondents how "coaches in my lacrosse community value" the above traits. Eighty-nine percent agreed or strongly agreed that teaching life lessons was essential. Ninety-six percent were in favor of the value of winning. Ninety-four percent of the sample believed that "instilling a love of the game was essential and 92 percent claimed that "honoring the game" is valued by coaches. When asked what non-coaching parents in my lacrosse commu-nity value, the results were very different: Teaching life lessons (85 percent), winning (96 percent), instilling a love of the game (79 percent), and honoring the game (74 percent). The instruc-tive lesson from this data is that coaches and non-coaching

Survey of Lacrosse Stakeholders		
Coaches and non-coaching parents in my community value:		
	Coaches Agree/Strongly Agree	Non-coaching parents Agree/Strongly Agree
Winning	96%	96%
Teaching Life Lessons	89%	85%
Instilling a love of the game	94%	79%
Honoring the game	92%	74%

parents may value different aspects of the experience. How does this difference translate to the players' experience, and what can we do to ensure consistent core values when reasonable people tend to differ?

If a team or program's core values are going to hold any traction, it is important that all participants know what they look like in action and be committed to making them come alive. A fellow high school lacrosse coach, who also happened to be a football coach, called me once to ask for advice on some disciplinary action taken with a group of football players. There were a significant number of players whose actions removed them from the team for the remainder of the season. I asked him what the core values of the team were. He said the team's core values were developed during pre-season camp. They were family, love and friendship. I then asked him how they related to the players' behavior. When the coaches individually asked these young men about their misdeeds, the majority of them replied, "If I had known that I would have gotten it trouble and eventually be thrown off the team . . . . I wouldn't have gotten caught! The mass response by the misguided players was very disturbing to the coaches, as well it should have been. In preparation for the following season, the team met with the coaches and all players "declared" themselves by developing a set of behavioral expectations and consequences. The team went to the state playoffs that season.

Core values are only words unless they can be observed in consistent action. Defined appropriately, a core value is understood by all members of the team, and as part of team membership, the core value represents a contract to play by the school/team rules. Developing and applying core values can be a consuming process that can seem like the administrative equivalent of chewing in foil. Putting words to action, and having all participants know and understand what these actions look like is no easy task. The use of "Five D's" can provide lacrosse programs with instructive assistance for putting core values into motion. First, there must be **D**ialogue in which the team and program stakeholders identify what core values they will live by. Second, it is important to develop a consensus in **D**efining these values –

stating clearly what each means to the success of the program and what each looks like. Core values must then be **D**econstructed – broken down to their simplest terms. In other words, what do these virtues look like behaviorally? Fourth, core values and their application must be **D**eclared by the group to be of prime importance. Finally, team and program participants must commit themselves to acting in accordance with these agreed-upon standards. They must go out and **D**o them!

The 5 D's of Lacrosse Core Value Construction

Dialogue — Identify

Define

Deconstruct — Know

Declare — Value

Do — Act

Al Rotatori, head boys' coach at Newton South High School, MA, youth lacrosse coach and former player for the University of Massachusetts and the Boston Blazers of the MILL, says, "I have coached for 17 years at the high school level and have coached against many different people. Our team schedule is a direct reflection of the coaches of the opposing team. In other words, I will not put a team, if I can help it, on my schedule if I don't think the opposing coach has the same important values about the games and competitions that I have."

The mission of US Lacrosse binds those involved in the game to a common purpose. As the whole is greater than the sum of its parts, it is essential that all stakeholder groups in all programs – players, coaches, administration, the industry, parents/spectators and officials – "declare" themselves in following the mission and core values of US Lacrosse. Embracing core values symbolizes the shared commitment of each group to "One Goal...Bringing Lacrosse to Life." US Lacrosse's core values were created by a variety of participants from all lacrosse constituencies in July 2004. These are seven cardinal traits that best represent the national governing body's approach to the game.

While lacrosse has experienced enormous growth, it had for many years remained small enough to have avoided the serious conflict of values and actions that have affected larger sports. However, as it continues to grow it is apparent now that all stakeholders need to be proactive in promoting the values that attracted us to the sport and US Lacrosse in the first place – values like: connection, leadership, respect, spirit, tradition, trust and youth.

Connection

> *We often use the metaphor of "connected by strings" to describe the synergy of teammates working together, with each player guiding the other. We do lots of visualization to help players focus on being in the moment, playing in the zone, free from any external distractions.*
>
> —Missy Foote, Head Women's Coach, Middlebury College

Lacrosse is made better when there is a common link and collaboration of players, coaches, players, administration, the industry, parents/spectators, and officials. The bond is two-fold. When this positive culture is established, players tend to better "connect the dots" on the field, as well as create and maintain healthy overall relationships on and off the field. "This is made between coaches and players that share a passion for the game. They both work together successfully to learn and improve," says Rob Quinn. An authentic connection between teammates, coaches, and others is achieved when there is an unspoken, yet understood, meaningful commitment and mutual respect to each other that goes to a deeper level. It is a feel and sharing of common values.

Wendy Kridel admits that the "connection" of the game is as simple as passing the ball up the field. It is all connected. Are you going to catch my pass? Or are you going to give it back to me? Instead of the give-and-go, will you take the shot? The collaboration on the field invites "instincts for your own game and for how your fellow teammates play so that you don't even react to them but anticipate. It increases the speed and the fluidity of the game," says Missy Foote. Respondents to the US Lacrosse survey claimed that "connection" is alive and well with 98 percent agreeing that lacrosse promotes cooperation and team cohesion.

The game becomes so much fun when you play with a group that you know will "get it done," says Brad Jorgenson. "The best teams I played with believed that every member of the squad would do their job, and do it well. There was never any doubt that our offense would score, our defense would dominate, or our goalie would stop the ball. Playing time was never questioned, because everybody was good, and everybody knew it. It almost turned players into spectators, but in a good way."

This experience is what we commonly call "team chemistry." "When players become so closely intertwined with a team it is hard to distinguish a single part from the whole," says Brad Nasato, assistant men's coach at Limestone College.

Steve Bristol says, "Lacrosse will always act as a link between individuals the same way that having gone to the same school will." This shared experience is part of the legacy that is enduring within teams and programs at all levels.

"The number of guys who have gone into coaching at the college and high school level from Springfield College is great. So many guys giving back to the game by becoming coaches is wonderful. I really feel it's the most rewarding part of my job," reflects Keith Bugbee.

"There is a great respect among the coaches, teammates and alums who have played the game at our school," says Chris Paradis. "When alums write or email about their lives and lacrosse, I share these ideas with my current players so that it will teach them the importance of respecting the long and very rich tradition. I receive calls with good wishes or congratulations from alums, especially prior to or after a big game."

The game is connected to life lessons and is learned on the playing field as much as in the classroom. Let lacrosse open the door to other opportunities. These are made between coaches and players that share a passion for the game. They both work together successfully to learn and improve. When we can keep a sense that we are all in it together we will be able to sustain positive growth.

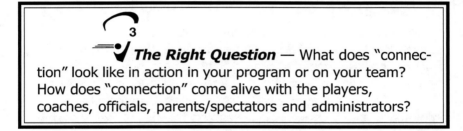

The Right Question — What does "connection" look like in action in your program or on your team? How does "connection" come alive with the players, coaches, officials, parents/spectators and administrators?

Leadership

Leadership in lacrosse is both a privilege and an opportunity. Leaders serve others in the sport by carrying and communicating a healthy vision and purpose for lacrosse participation and by setting a meaningful example. Program and team leadership stem from those adults who have committed to serving those in their charge. Coaches, team captains, parents, officials and administrators all have a stake in the players' lacrosse experience.

Lacrosse can also be an instructive activity to bring leadership to the life of its players. Eighty-six percent of the survey sample indicated that they participate in lacrosse "to develop leadership skills." It is interesting that the greatest percentage of respondents who either agree or strongly agree with this statement are girls' interscholastic (91 percent); women's college (96 percent), and women's intercollegiate associates (90 percent) as compared to high school boys (84 percent), men's college (85 percent) and men's intercollegiate associates (77 percent).

3

☑ *The Right Question* — What does "leadership" look like in action in your program or on your team? How does "leadership" come alive with the players, coaches, officials, parents/spectators and administrators?

Respect

All people matter in the game. Respect for others in the lacrosse community and beyond means treating teammates, coaches, opposing teams, officials and fans as you wish to be treated, with unconditional positive regard. Honoring the game with fair and safe play provides the greatest opportunity for enjoyment, satisfaction and success on the field. "Respect permeates the game at all levels, beginning with a respect for the tradition of the game, and extending to a respect for anyone involved...player, coach, official, school club...etc. Maintenance of the tradition requires respect for it," says Steve Bristol.

"I think that it has to be respecting yourself, respecting your coach, respecting your opponent, but more importantly respecting the game," says Wendy Kridel. "I see this weakening. It is upsetting to me. When players jump every whistle or intentionally hold players trying to cut, this is not in the spirit of the game at all. When an official is having a bad game and all of a sudden you can't play above what's happening and keep your mind free and be able to play, regardless of the officiating, it really has an impact on what's happening. It is the truth. Different coaches take it different ways. I think that there are many people who don't even consider that phrase. What do you mean by respecting the game? 'I am out here coaching kids and working my butt off trying to win games.' You can't convince somebody that they would be better served by respecting the game."

This declaration of respect is supported by the Positive Coaching Alliance (a partner of US Lacrosse):

Coaches feel the responsibility not only to teach their players the skills and strategy behind the game but also a respect for the tradition of the game and for all who are involved (teammates, opponents, officials, and fans). Learning to honor the game contributes to a growing sense of responsibility and maturing moral reasoning that helps athletes prepare to become contributing citizens of the larger community.

The Golden Rule states that we ought to treat everyone the way we want to be treated. "Some coaches seem to lose this as they try to get every advantage and look for a scapegoat when things go wrong. Unfortunately, some fans miss this all the time," says Jim Tighe, a long-time men's official and member of the New England Lacrosse Hall of Fame. John Hill, a college official and also a member of the New England Hall of Fame, agrees that respect "MUST go on between the lines for every game for the game to be made better. Unfortunately, it does not always happen."

All participants ought to be taken seriously, not only as lacrosse players, but also as well-rounded people in their own right. Regardless of ability and talent, Alan McCoy says it is important "to respect that a full life includes many elements that are not lacrosse, and as a coach or program director, keep lacrosse in balance so that the participants can develop as whole people." Respect in all aspects of life is earned as much as it is offered. Respect is harder to earn than disrespect. This is why it is coveted. Anyone involved with the game in any way and at any level is an asset to lacrosse. Wanting to see others succeed and recognizing them when they do is a gift we deserve to receive and also give.

Part of the whole respect "package" includes competing against opponents with our skills, tactics and with our hearts. Depending on their introduction to lacrosse, or to any other sport for that matter, respecting opponents may be a foreign idea for many young athletes. When programs are run with integrity and an obvious command for respect, most players eventually begin to "get it."

John Piper says, "Respect for teammates, the officials and the other team are among the values I reinforce with my players. It amazes me how many people will blame a loss on the ref. The game was probably lost in the first quarter not in the last quarter. It is not the last play that does it. I keep telling the kids that we win as a team and we lose as a team. Games are sometimes won before you step on the field based on frame of mind."

Shaun Stanton, head boys' coach at St. Sebastian High School, MA, believes an exciting, enduring part of the game is the development of respect for one's opponent, as this player may be your teammate another day. Scores of young players eventually play on the same team with former opponents, and many high school players find themselves on the same field, but in different uniforms, as former teammates.

Keith Bugbee echoes the importance of his players respecting those who have played before at Springfield. "I want my players to appreciate the Springfield College lacrosse tradition."

Lou Corsetti, a member of US Lacrosse's Youth Council and director of boys' youth programs in Atlanta, has created a great tag line – "You are in the game." When players, coaches, parents/spectators, officials and administrators "declare" themselves to respect the game, they become full-fledged participants. Being "in the game" means that you consistently exhibit respect for everyone involved in the game. John Buxton, head of school at The Culver Academies and a former attackman at Brown in the late 1960s, says that it is disturbing when coaches refer to the opposing team by saying, "They don't deserve to belong on the same field with you." Although a coach may be trying his or her best to motivate the team with these assumptions and accusations, we owe our players and the opponents a level of "human" respect regardless of ability and talent.

3

☑ *The Right Questions* — What does "respect" look like in action in your program or on your team? How does "respect" come alive with players, coaches, officials, parents/spectators and administrators?

Spirit

Spirit is a fundamental emotional principle through which participants bring the excitement of the game to life by way of vigor, loyalty and dedication. Spirit describes the joy of the game, which is a by-product of all of the other US Lacrosse core values – connection, leadership, respect, tradition, trust and commitment to youth. It is also the ability to play with "single-pointed attention," free from distractions which unlocks one's spirit and allows one to move beyond ones focus of right and wrong. Hall of Fame umpire Susie Ganzenmuller believes spirit "is the essence, soul or the main principle governing a game to keep it fair and safe, and team spirit is an energy that binds or invigorates the team." Team spirit is energy that binds or invigorates the team. Similarly, there is a "spirit" of competition in lacrosse that is unique. The spirit follows from the respect of the participants for the game and each other. The spirit is the common bond that lacrosse creates amongst and between its participants.

Following comments made in Chapter 1, the game has a tradition that transcends its history. Steve Bristol says, "the spirit of the game is a feeling of honor and dignity that I associate with the game." Similarly, there is a "spirit" of competition in lacrosse that is unique. The spirit follows from the respect of the partici-pants for the game and each other. The spirit is the common bond that lacrosse creates amongst and between its participants." Rob Quinn believes "spirit" is the element that separates the great players from the good players, and the great coaches from the good coaches. Those who possess this sixth sense in lacrosse display this undeniable trait. It's part enthusiasm and part passion that combine to create that spirit – a passion and drive that boosts the play of those involved.

Spirit is the essence of an experience; the force that takes something beyond our normal understanding. "It is something that is greater than any single game or individual. It is the essence of an experience; the force that takes something beyond our normal understanding," says Brad Nasato.

Wendy Kridel agrees, "It is the love of the game. The first thing that I think of when you say spirit is just fun, joy. I immediately picture kids in their school colors. It is something that, at a girls' school, you are always working towards, being spirited and showing your spirit. Your spirit is really who you are. It is that feeling you get on that first really sunny day in pre-season."

"Lacrosse is not just a game to me, but a way of life," says Al Rotatori, head boys coach at Newton South High School, MA. Lacrosse has given me a meaning and purpose in life. Except for my family, it is the only place where I really feel comfortable, secure and needed. When I step onto the field, whether to play or coach, I have a feeling of calmness and confidence."

Many interviewees on the men's side of the game fondly spoke of the legendary Peter Kohn as an icon of the "spirit" of the game. He was the legendary manager of many teams, including the 1982 U.S. men's team. Although I was unsuccessful in my bid to make the team, I distinctly remember getter a rap on my door at tryouts every morning at 7 a.m., announcing, "Time to make the World Team." Peter's affirmations represent a living, breathing "spirit of the game" in many of us. The spirit was alive and well when he was inducted in the Lacrosse Hall of Fame in November 2004. His enthusiasm and dedication to the game has inspired many of us.

Spirit is our passion and the drive that keeps us playing and involved. Without spirit, lacrosse is without tradition and culture. Jeff Long, former US Men's team member and current head men's coach at Ithaca College says, "The nature of the game nurtures the soul of the player. Play with your heart and head and your body will follow, usually with positive results!"

⌒
3
✓ The Right Questions — What does "spirit" look like in action in your program or on your team? How does "spirit" come alive with players, coaches, officials, parents/spectators and administrators?

Tradition

Lacrosse tradition is composed of the valuable stories, customs and rituals that are passed down from generation to generation. Although change is inevitable as the game grows, it is essential to maintain the enduring tenets that serve as a foundation to the quality of the game. As mentioned in Chapter 1, the development of "tradition" is an enduring anchor that, to this point, has withstood the test of time. This anchor allows participants to continue their quest for a quality lacrosse experience. The important principles of the past are related to what is happening in the present. Tradition is based on consistency of action in keeping the sport alive.

Lacrosse's unique tradition has a special place in the game. We need to keep that out front for all the people who are relative newcomers to the game. By honoring those who have come before, the history and unique values associated with the program are honored. Lacrosse tradition always emphasizes playing the game the "right" way. Thus, we protect and honor the game with reverence, respect, and passion. The overarching Native American tradition can also be transferred into specific team culture.

"I think every player should know who started this great game and respect the heritage," says Rob Quinn. "We try to incorporate that in our program. Then I think each school should have their own traditions that pay respect to those who came before them. In the overall game I feel we've lost the tradition of sportsmanship. There is far too much trash talking and disrespecting of officials in today's game. Much more than there was decades ago."

The Value of Tradition

As a varsity high school head coach, I spent more time developing attitude and an approach to the game. We have as our school mascot the Hurricanes. Twenty years ago, I purchased a set of hurricane warning flags that are placed behind our bench for every home game. Our team has developed a Native American chant that we shout out before we take the field to start a game. I would bring out Native American trivia questions at the beginning or end of each practice. We utilize the sacred Native American colors to designate our midfield lines – red, black, white, and yellow. Also we use various weather conditions to designate different units – such as tornados are the face-off units, cyclones are the man-up offensive units, storm unit is our defensive unit. Our goalie is the "Keeper of the Flame." Zephyrs are the attackmen; Tsunamis are the man-down midfield defensive unit. Also, we use the terms monsoon and gale-force.

When we chat about taking a day off for the weekend the players are reminded that there is no "firewater" and/or "communicating with our ancestors" – i.e. no smoking or other drugs. When we start every game the team is reminded of the famous Apache proverb – "It is better to have less thunder in the mouth, and more lightning in the hand."

The players like and appreciate the "weather-culture" and the "Native-American" culture that we utilize with our team. It has truly developed a strong sense of pride. It is truly our "Hurricane Lacrosse tradition."

—Larry Briggs, Former Head Boys' Coach, Amherst High School, MA

For whatever reason, the history of lacrosse has remained a significant part of the sport. Every lacrosse player can tell stories (some of which might even be true) of how the game began with the Native Americans. Steve Bristol elaborates, "Perhaps it is because for so long lacrosse was a relatively unknown sport. Participation was like being a part of a unique club, and part of your responsibility as a participant was knowing something about the history. An additional responsibility for participants was a respect for the game. Again, my guess is that this results from it having been a relatively unknown sport for many people. Each player carried a larger burden of responsibility due to the few number of participants. In other sports, you don't feel the sense of ownership that one does in lacrosse."

It is essential that the core value of tradition be embraced and reinforced in youth programs as a means of connection, enjoyment and playing the game the way it was designed to be played. Jay Williams says, "Tradition has been diluted since I was introduced to the game many years ago. It was emphasized by coaches, drilled in a game – a great game – to sustain itself if people give back to it. What will the attitudes of many 10- and 20-year olds involved in the game be in 20 years when they are our youth, high school and college coaches?"

3

The Right Questions — What does "tradition" look like in action in your program or on your team? How does "tradition" come alive with players, coaches, officials, parents/spectators and administrators?

Trust

Trust is a gift that can't be bought, an assurance that can't be required of anyone; it's born of long acquaintance and mutual respect. If someone has to ask for our trust, then the person is not sure he or she deserves it. And if we find that we need to say "Oh, it's okay, I trust you," then probably we don't.

— Lee Smith, *Trust*

Trust is having faith and confidence in others in the lacrosse community. Everyone has a role, whether coach, official, player or other contributor, and must be trusted and empowered to perform the duties of that role. Trust is an essential trait to all healthy relationships, be it on or off the lacrosse field. When I talk about healthy relationships in my classes, I always ask the students what they believe to be one of the most important traits. As you probably have read so far (and I am preaching to the choir), trust is a foundation to a quality lacrosse experience that invites increased mastery, performance, and overall relational satisfaction and enjoyment. If we believe the best about people—teammates, opposing coaches and players, officials and parents, we find that this is always true.

"Trust must exist between teammates and coaches for a team to be successful," said Steve Bristol. "As a player, I need to trust my teammate to do his job, and then simply worry about doing mine. When that happens all over a field, the collaboration of teammates outlined above occurs, and the proverbial stars align."

Terry Mangan, head men's coach at Lafayette College agrees. "Trust is the essence of a team; when a player works and sacrifices he can count on his teammates to demand the same from themselves." By their very nature, both the men's and women's games invite players of different positions to trust each other when the ball transitions from offense to defense and back to offense.

It is also important for the player to have the ability to feel free to know that the adults – coaches, officials, parents and administrators – are making the right decision on their behalf – in most situations. This is important regarding safety and other physical and emotional aspects.

When trust exists between teammates and coaches, a team has a greater opportunity to succeed. For example, a player needs to trust his or her teammates to do their job, and then simply worry about doing his or her best. This is putting faith in each other to work one's hardest to excel. "Because each person trusts her teammates' ability to play their role, she can focus on playing her role," says Missy Foote. "With the quick passing of lacrosse there is no opportunity for a one-person show, so teamwork and trust are so essential."

However, when a player or coach is distracted, even for a brief moment, because he or she may not fully trust the actions of another teammate, coach, official or parent, then performance may be compromised on the field. If there is enough doubt in the participant's mind, then his or her focus is not on the task at hand. "Trust means believing the best about people: players, opposing coaches and players, officials, parents. We are all finding our own way and most people have honorable intentions, even if we often fall short in pursuit of our goals," says Alan McCoy.

Officials and opposing coaches ought to be able to trust the coach who certifies that his or her players are properly equipped. And coaches ought to be able to trust their players to have the proper and legal equipment. The certification is a verbal contract that binds the respect that should be accorded to both teams. When we trust that all players intentionally enter the field of play with a stick that has a legal pocket and length, we set the game up to be played the way it is supposed to be. However, if a player hasn't prepared well and tries to equal the playing field by using an illegal stick, then he or she hasn't established the trust in him or herself to be "freed" up to play well. Good officials trust their ability to call the game properly, and just as importantly, they share a trust in their partner's ability. "As an official, I have to trust in my ability to call the game properly, and most important, I need to trust my partners," says John Hill.

Many coaches who were interviewed believe that "trust is interwoven in everything we do with our program." Adults are the proverbial bus drivers. They drive the notion that trust is essential in the game. This happens when coaches believe in players, and players believe in teammates to do the right thing. They ask the important question of themselves and each other: Will my action(s) be good or bad for my team, knowing that we ought to do what is right no matter what our feelings?

It can take time to earn this level of trust, of unconditional positive regard for other. But it is time well spent, especially for young athletes as they navigate their development as lacrosse players and good human beings.

⌐ 3

☑ **The Right Questions** — What does "trust" look like in action in your program or on your team? How does "trust" come alive with players, coaches, officials, parents/spectators and administrators?

Commitment to Youth

A commitment to the proper development of youth programs is critical, as youth represents the future of the game and holds its legacy in their hands. It is essential that the lacrosse community honor the privilege and responsibility it has in interacting with young players during this maturational time. We need to reinvest in great youth coaches.

Renewal is important to all of life's ventures, and as we welcome youth and new adult coaches into the game, it is important for more experienced coaches and parents to accept their roles as mentors to help sustain the remarkable tradition of sportsmanship, camaraderie and fair play.

This renewal is important to all of life's ventures and helps to continue the life cycle. As we bring youth into the game, it is important to plant the seed early – teach them about traditions, talk about respect, and the development of trust. We help young players learn to love the game earlier on.

It is a wonderful gift for adults to introduce and share this game with young people. Youth lacrosse is educated fun with an emphasis on providing a pleasant learning environment. Youth players, for the most part, bring an open mind, body and spirit. It is important to connect with their vibrant nature by informing, educating and enabling, but not overly directing. The youth won't always be the youth. Nurture them and it will pay dividends. One coach says, "I just think of young kids having fun. When I think of youth and how I tie it to the game, I just picture these third graders with sticks that are really long and mouth-guards that they are gagging on because they won't take it out. Not having a clue but just wanting to be out there. Trying new stuff and just really and purely having fun."

3

✓ The Right Questions — What does a commitment to "youth" look like in action in your program or on your team? How does the commitment to "youth" come alive with players, coaches, officials, parents/spectators and administrators?

When John Pirani became the head coach at Winchester, he set a few goals for the program and himself. Those were the days before the proliferation of youth lacrosse, and he really wanted to build a youth program. "We started youth lacrosse with the help of many hard-working people, some of whom were my teammates when I was a player and others some very nice parents of younger players in town," he says. "Our first chore was to develop a constitution that ensured younger players were well treated."

It is important to work with other adults who understand how to make provisions for the fair and ethical treatment of kids and create teams that can compete, but not at the expense of maximum participation. Pirani claims, "When we wrote that first constitution, we had no idea that it would serve as a model for other programs that came along later. It was simple, really. We just wrote down what we had experienced in lacrosse. It never really occurred to us that we were taking an unusual position relative to the experiences of other sports."

As time passes, however, it is clear that elite play, travel teams and cuts at the youth sports level have proliferated in other sports. "Our goal was to ensure that every boy and girl would be able to play lacrosse in a comfortable, safe place. The vision of how a good youth program should be run ought to be a mirror of our experiences, hopes and vision for how boys should access lacrosse," says Pirani.

What becomes clear is that no one element of the program exists independently of any other part. A safe place for kids to play as youngsters, community service high school aged coaches, a committed and responsible set of teams at the high school level all are dependent upon one another. If any element breaks down, it becomes obvious, and the remedies are usually modeled in the other, well functioning elements. Visions, commitment, excellence in motives all are embedded in every element of the community and program, and in each individual team. Bringing those qualities to the players is easy because none are discordant with good practices across any level of play.

Chapter 4

The Art of Good Coaching and Officiating

Successful coaches build a culture of trust and honesty so players believe in what they are being taught. Good coaches instinctively know how team members are going to play together, and building trust enables them to improve individually and collectively.

—Kristen Aceto Corrigan, Former U.S. National Team player; Head Coach, Culver Girls Academy

The formation of good character and individual and team strategy execution doesn't happen in a vacuum. It more often than not appears when good coaches take the risk to be fully present in their work with lacrosse players. Good lacrosse coaches and other adult mentors know how to teach the game, whether they've ever played it or not. They are mentors, modelers and managers; they understand the abilities of players and present techniques and strategies that players are capable of understanding and applying; they are effective and efficient in teaching skills and habits; and they provide an environment that expands on the player's range of experiences.

However, there continues to be a tension in most sports' cultures, lacrosse included, with coaches who prefer performance or mastery climates. The performance environment equates success with won-loss records, where there isn't an emphasis on participant enjoyment and satisfaction as a major outcome. A healthy blend of both environments is the aspiration of a "double goal coach" – mentors who are in the business of "performance" and also support the "mastery" of skills, relationships, etc.

Lacrosse Coaches as Mentors, Modelers and Managers

Mentoring

Good coaches are mentors to many of their players. The consistency of the coachs' actions and words speaks volumes to the care that is directed towards the player. Sam Osherson, a psychologist who specializes in mentor relationships, suggests that by "showing up and being there" for young people, mentoring is mutually beneficial to both the player and the coach. Coaches, through their sharing of experience and wisdom, receive the chance for reflection on the reciprocal influences of the coach-player relationship. Mentoring done "right" allows the player to see the coach as being fully human, not some sacred icon to be revered or demon to be exorcised.

Carol Hotchkiss, of the Durango Institute in Colorado, claims that the "moment of connection" between a resistant young person and a caring adult may be acknowledged in a concealed manner without ever having a lengthy dialogue. As good coaches and mentors, we must trust the risks we take to open our hearts to our challenging players. Our brief encounters with them cannot be evaluated in a win/loss column. All we can hope for is to have them realize their responsibilities and opportunities through playing lacrosse.

It is not uncommon for good coaches to realize the influence that have on others as mentors. John Piper, the head boys' lacrosse coach at North Carroll High in the rural foothills northwest of Baltimore, was surprised and amazed to read an essay written about his "mentorship" by one of his players. John claimed that he didn't realize the influence he had on this young man's life.

The Pied Piper

A significant leader in my life has been my lacrosse coach. My coach has pushed me on and off the field to be a better person and has taught me to strive to be the best. Along with the team he works with me one on one and helps me when I need him the most. He led me to achieving my goals and becoming a leader. On the field, my sophomore year, I was awarded the defensive Most Valuable Player award and was selected to be the captain of the team for multiple games. Off the field he has pushed me for high academic achievement. A few days this year he has taken his time to sit down with my parents and me to help plan for my future. He has helped me with my college planning and my career goals.

Not only does he help me, but he also helps others. He puts in extra time whenever he can to help anyone in need. He is one of the teachers in charge of the Varsity Club of North Carroll. In the fall he is the only person willing to supervise the weight room. He encourages his team to lift and run to stay in shape in the off-season. Not only does he open it for his team, but also for anyone else who wants to use it. He pushes the team for excellence in academics as well as athletics. He holds study halls before practice a few times a week so everyone has time to get their school work done. When someone is behind in a class or needs extra help from his teacher, Coach is understanding and lets him meet with whomever he needs to. His study halls resulted in a team with high academics. Only a few team members received report cards with less than all A's and B's. Along with coaching he teaches special education, which I feel is a tough and strenuous job. He works with kids who each have a different problem that needs special attention like not being able to walk, talk, or even eat on their own. He shows patience and never gets frustrated when they need his help. On top of all this he has a family at home, a wife and four kids, to whom he gives his full attention. Even with his busy schedule, he always manages to spend time with his family, students, and team.

These qualities as a person, I feel make him a great leader. He always seems to manage his time wisely. He makes everyone a better person. He is someone who I look up to and admire, and would like to become. Seeing how he touches the lives of others, I would like to be able to do the same. This is why he is my leader and someone I look up to.

—Justin Drobitch, Lacrosse Player, North Caroll High School, MD

Good mentoring also includes the ability to "live in the skin" of your players – to really know what the elations and frustrations are like for them. Bob Stevenson has coached girls' youth lacrosse in the Washington, DC area for years. He believes that patience is a key at the youth level. Lacrosse is a challenging sport to pick up at the beginning (different than soccer), since it is a skilled game that requires a chain of movements. As a patient motivator he says, "Girls do not respond to yelling as well as they respond to positive reinforcement."

Shaped by Coaches and Family

Kim Simons, my former coach at Georgetown, has made a significant difference in my life decisions. She has been with me through a lot. We have been together for six years playing and three years coaching. It's certainly a pretty significant time period in my life. She gave me an opportunity to play here, to dream about and practically win the national championship. Then she gave me the opportunity to come back and coach. It was an opportunity I hadn't even considered but she knew that this would be something that I would love. So she is by far the most influential person. I was introduced to lacrosse in middle school at the Windsor School in Boston. They certainly have a special place in my heart because they introduced me to the game. My high school coach, Kathy Noche, was not only a great coach but a very good friend and a great person. I think that my family is certainly a big part of that as well in terms of allowing me to follow my passion and support me along the way. They allowed me to do what I wanted to do and helped me deal with the fact the people say 'What else do you do?' when I say that I coach. That has been a big part of it. Kevin Hicks, Sean Quirk and John Yeager have certainly been a big part of my consideration of playing in college.

—Bowen Holden, Head Women's Coach, Boston College

Being patient and positive is a great formula to making the game fun and this becomes contagious with the kids as they build their skills. "Constant positive reinforcement at youth, middle and high school girl's lacrosse is essential," says Jessica Battle, head girls' coach at Coronado High School in San Diego. She says it is important to address that girls play lacrosse for a variety of reasons. "Some girls between third and eighth grade may be a bit more emotionally delicate/fragile. Some girls are still tomboys. Some are participating for social reasons because their friends are, or perhaps they are involved because their parents want them to play." It is also essential that men who coach girls have a strong understanding of the psychology of female adolescents.

Modeling

Good coaches are also influential modelers of behavior. Through their ideals, words and actions, they set the example of "leading by deed." That is why good coaching consists of teaching athletes a number of small chains of consistent skill sets that help the athletes produce a variety of complex motions. Lacrosse players also observe the consistency of the coach – they are very alert to adult hypocrisy. Adolescents respond strongly to adults who are clear about their adult responsibilities and appear to have influence. To a coach who has a well-formed character, this isn't even an issue. These actions are so habituated, that to do otherwise would never enter into the picture. Coaches can take advantage of teachable moments by displaying behaviors in difficult situations they would like their players to imitate. The coach should ask him or herself, "If the players on my team are a mirror of my actions, what do I see in the reflection?"

Some parents have instilled positive moral values in their children, as evidenced by the strong character traits they develop by high school. As high school coaches, we spend so much time with our players, we should reinforce what they have been taught with every action we take. "Hard work, commitment and dedication will be mirrored by our athletes; as will cheating, cutting corners, swearing, or any negative attributes if the athlete has not developed his true character," says Gene Zanella. High school students are struggling to develop their own character identity and are looking for role models wherever they can be found.

Erin Quinn has received numerous coaching awards and epitomizes the ideal of good mentoring and modeling. However, Erin never played lacrosse. After an outstanding undergraduate football career at Middlebury, he spent a great deal of time learning the technical and tactical components of the game under the tutelage of then head coach Jim Grube. After serving as graduate assistant and assistant coach, he eventually became head coach. Erin's ability to model the behavioral expectations of his team — by having a solid knowledge of the game and a well-formed character — attracts many aspiring student-athletes to this serene campus in the mountains of Vermont.

Dave Campbell, an All-American goalie who played for Quinn and is now the head men's coach at Connecticut College says, "Coach Quinn set a great example for his players in how he conducted himself on a day to day basis. He was also very clear in what was and wasn't acceptable if you were going to be a part of that program. He was not a hard head about it, but everyone just knew how to do the right thing. As a by-product of how we did things on a day to day basis we were able to do pretty well with the wins and losses. I do believe that teams with great character have an advantage in game situations when the intensity gets cranked up a notch. They are less likely to get on each other, to start blaming the official, to get down on themselves. A player with good character reacts to his own performance in a consistent manner whether he makes a good or bad play — whether the goal is scored for or against his team, or the call went the other way. I do think that makes a difference at any level, but more so at the higher level of play."

Managing

Good coaches see the big picture and keep the projector in focus as they manage the jigsaw puzzle of responsibilities in serving their athletes. When coaches lose sight of the mission, it puts stress on the program. Good programs don't explode and become bad programs — instead they fray. Managing the process, which includes following the program's mission, is no easy task. It requires consistent supervision and evaluation.

John Pirani believes that coaching management is one of the keys to enjoyment and improved performance. The field is the coach's classroom and the same level of control needs to be established. Bob Bigelow, a youth sports advocate and the author of "Just Let the Kids Play," believes that managing young people is a key to their enjoyment and satisfaction. And the best coaches create this healthy environment to enhance performance so that people in the organization can do their best work with the least amount of distraction. Good coaches create a daily set of conditions. Mark Boyea, former athletic director of The Montclair Kimberley Academy, claims that a "performance-conducive" environment is one within which distractions are minimized for the players, allowing them to direct an optimal degree of their physical, mental and emotional resources to the task at hand on the field.

Traits of Successful Lacrosse Coaches

Boyea claims that for every 100 different coaches, there are 100 different styles. Research hasn't been able to prove that any specific style works best. However, successful coaches seem to possess the four following traits: purpose, competence in teaching technical and strategic skills, the ability to relate positively to student-athletes, and a well-formed character.

Purpose – Vision

Missy Foote realizes that most coaches will not say that they measure success by wins and losses, but a successful coach should have helped her team play better than it did when it was first formed, and helped each player find her own "greatness." It is a coach's responsibility to inspire and guide her players, and that should translate into a feeling of success from her players. A successful coach must be honest and loyal and treat her players with respect, and she should expect the same of them.

Brad Nasato claims that success can mean many different things. He alludes, "I think success is achieving something that makes you happy, while at the same time benefiting those around you in some way. Successful coaches are often measured by wins. However, a successful coach, along with winning, must also be able to motivate his players to perform to the best of their abilities, thus benefiting the coach and other team members. In order to achieve those goals a coach must first and foremost be a good leader. He or she must make the tough decisions and stand by them regardless of the situation.

Jeff Long says, "They are motivators – making everyone on the team feel important to the cause, being fair yet maybe not equal. Different athletes sometimes require a different approach."

"A successful coach knows his/her players and what motivates them", says Dee Stephan. When players believe in themselves and realize they can accomplish great things, they play as a team. This vision gets the players to love the game, have fun, learn and give back.

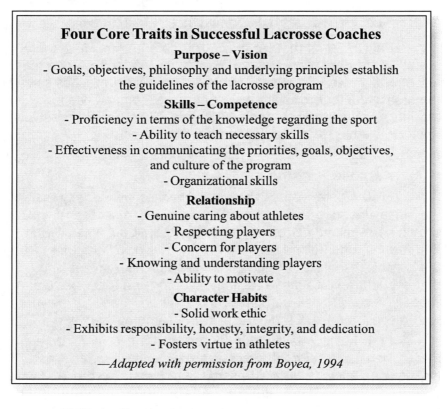

Four Core Traits in Successful Lacrosse Coaches

Purpose – Vision
- Goals, objectives, philosophy and underlying principles establish the guidelines of the lacrosse program

Skills – Competence
- Proficiency in terms of the knowledge regarding the sport
- Ability to teach necessary skills
- Effectiveness in communicating the priorities, goals, objectives, and culture of the program
- Organizational skills

Relationship
- Genuine caring about athletes
- Respecting players
- Concern for players
- Knowing and understanding players
- Ability to motivate

Character Habits
- Solid work ethic
- Exhibits responsibility, honesty, integrity, and dedication
- Fosters virtue in athletes

—Adapted with permission from Boyea, 1994

Skills – Competence

Successful coaches are able to teach effectively and have strong communication and organizational skills. He or she must know the X's and O's of the game and be able to teach those to the players. He or she must be able to react quickly and effectively under pressure and adversity. "Good coaches possess a core knowledge of the game and ability to express this knowledge in a clear and concise manner," says Jeff Long. They have confidence in themselves to direct and take responsibility for such actions, for talent evaluation, for recognizing strengths and weaknesses of individuals and being able to improve on both in a positive manner.

Prior to coaching at Amherst College, Chris Paradis mentored athletes at a secondary independent school. She recalls that some of the college coaches who had some of her former players said, "I can tell she is one of yours." They realized that her graduates played and carried the ball similar to how she played. "That was a turning point for me as a coach," says Chris. "To be able to do both – to teach athletes how to play and have them go on and play in college – is a wonderful compliment."

"In order to get to that level of success, it necessitates a high quality of preparation during the off-season and at each individual in-season practice," says Gordy Webb. "During games it is then necessary to elevate (yet control) your emotions so that you elicit your optimal level of energy, skill and decisions. If you can get yourself and your players to this point individually and collectively, the wins and losses will take care of themselves."

Relationship – Mattering

John Pirani believes that successful coaches are caring, knowledgeable communicators. He says, "On the face of it that seems simple. I think as a younger coach, I was fixated on strategy more than anything else. I'm sure that was because I was insecure and felt the need to demonstrate my knowledge and ability. I really didn't see myself as a caregiver, leader or role model until much later in my career. While there is no doubt that strategy is an important part of what we do, all the 'other stuff' tends to be far more important in terms of being successful. For that matter, 'success' is far broader than merely calculating wins and losses. Once I got that part straight in my head, winning and losing became easier. As a serious competitor, I don't mean to say that losing became easy, rather it is that I can be more comfortable with a loss if I know I have taken care of all the details that lead up to game day. While there have been days we have been beaten because I have been out-strategized, I don't believe that anyone outworks me or my staff when it comes to working with the whole student-athlete."

Ricky Fried claims that having competent knowledge of the game goes without saying at the highest level. He believes that good coaches have the ability to teach a player not only the skills but something about themselves. The coach should be able to adapt to different players and different ways of learning. Fried says, "I have 28 kids that we may be trying to teach something 20 different ways. The ability to adapt to the individual and to relate to that player and get them to trust you, not necessarily that you know what you are talking about but so that they can put themselves out to take chances and risks and learn about themselves is key. They are not going to do that unless they trust us." A successful coach must be able to read the personalities of his or her players and treat them accordingly to get the most out of them.

From a youth lacrosse perspective, Jay Williams says that, "Good coaches are really focused on the kids. They understand them as individuals and get to know them by developing a rapport and communication. Once this is accomplished, you can teach them almost anything."

It is a wonderful gift to teach athletes about life, decision-making and responsibility. It is gratifying for most coaches to be remembered as somebody who listens, who holds them accountable, and helps them learn life lessons by teaching them how to work together – teammates and friendship. This all ought to happen by "keeping the bar high while still keeping the respect." It isn't an either/or situation.

Character Habits

The US Lacrosse survey indicates that 96 percent of the sample agreed or strongly agreed that lacrosse coaches and other important adults exhibit strong character habits and help to

Everything is Relational

I think the relationships that you make are the most important thing to anyone who is involved on any level, either as a player or as a coach. I think that's what stays with you. Our field hockey coach is getting nominated for an award so she had to figure out her overall record. So I decided I would figure out mine. We looked at the number of games I coached as a high school coach and I coached about 200-250 games. I could probably tell you about a handful of them, where I really remember the game. I can tell you about every team I coached though. The kids on every team. I can remember this group of kids and I can place dates together and figure they graduated together about this time and where are they now. So it is all of that that really stays with you. If you take it from a playing perspective, yes, you have the relationships with each other, and you are always trying to say things like you don't have to be their friend you just have to respect each other. Most of the successful teams really are very tight but they don't have to be. It's the relationship that they have with their coach that is important as well.

—*Wendy Kridel, Head Coach Bryn Mawr School, PA*
US Women's Under-19 Head Coach

foster them in their players. "It is essential that these abilities are anchored by a strong foundation and that foundation is one of good character. If we, as coaches, do not meet the highest standards of character and values then we are perpetuating that substandard culture onto generations of young men and women that we have the privilege of coaching," says Brad Nasato.

"I'd say honesty, diligence, good sportsmanship and knowledge would be four essential characteristics," says Walter Alessi, long time head men's coach at the Massachusetts Institute of Technology. "You must be honest with your players. You must work hard and demand that they do also. And you must know enough about the game to teach it to others. If your players trust you, work hard and are taught properly, they will have a great experience regardless of the won-loss record."

Survey of Lacrosse Stakeholders

Lacrosse coaches and other important adults exhibit responsibility, honesty, integrity and dedication, and foster these characteristics in players.

		Number of Responses	Response Ratio
Strongly Agree	▬▬▬▬▬	*708*	*41%*
Agree	▬▬▬▬▬▬	*949*	*55%*
Disagree	▪	*69*	*4%*
Strongly Disagree		*5*	*0%*
	Total	*1731*	*100%*

"I think a coach is crucial to a player's character formation at all levels," says Mike Caravana, head boys' coach at Woodberry Forest, VA, and former head coach at Denison. "Doing things correctly and respecting the game is clearly on the shoulders of the head coach."

Gene Zanella believes the essential characteristics of a successful coach are "commitment, dedication, effort, knowledge and enthusiasm for lacrosse. A successful coach is an extremely suc-

Coach as Character Educator

I try to teach lifelong guidelines when I coach. I teach trustworthiness, truthfulness, active listening, no put-downs and give your personal best. These guidelines set the stage for a friendly environment. I also stress the importance of life skills. The life skills I include in my coaching philosophy include caring, common sense, cooperation, courage, curiosity, effort, flexibility, friendship, initiative, integrity, organization, patience, perseverance, pride, problem solving, resourcefulness, responsibility and a sense of humor. I feel passionate about lacrosse because I learned these skills through my association with lacrosse. These are the traits and characteristics that make lacrosse players successful.

—*Paul Sieben, Head Girls' Coach, St. Ursula's Academy, Toledo, OH*

cessful individual, who will definitely put the team members before himself. A successful season should never be measured solely on wins and losses, but team morale, fun, camaraderie; esprit de corps of the team should gauge its success. Winning will help make these, but a successful coach will be able to instill these values without wins."

Sid Jamieson claims that a successful coach has a total understanding of what his or her environment is, and is able to work within that particular environment with people who want to have success.

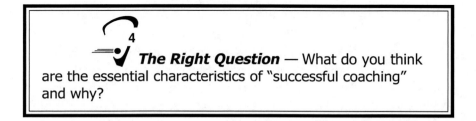

The Right Question — What do you think are the essential characteristics of "successful coaching" and why?

Lacrosse Coaching Styles

In my travels with coaches at all levels in all sports, especially in lacrosse, I have come to see a continuum and overlapping of styles. At one end we see the coach who has strengths in command/control – instructions are clear and are fulfilled by the players. The main focus is on making sure every aspect of skill and team strategy is accounted for. The servant leader coach understands that his or her responsibility is to derive mastery and performance characteristics and to ensure that the player's needs are taken care of. He or she seeks first to serve players – to make sure the needs of players are taken care of so they can perform as well as possible. Third, the composer/conductor acts as a consultant as the team takes care of business on the field. He or she is "available" to provide advice and counsel. Akin to an orchestra's brass, woodwinds, percussion and string sections, all players know their roles and responsibilities for their specific positions on the field, and their continuous interactions with the other positions. The coach waves his or her proverbial wand as the conductor, and welcomes discussion with players as a consultant. We can liken this to a successful clear culminating in a scoring opportunity.

It is important to note that each of these styles are not designed to be an either/or. Also, they are not considered to be a stage process. It is very possible, even probable, that many coaches will integrate all three of these styles at times. Some coaches spend the majority of time as command/controllers, while other split their time evenly among the three styles. It is important, that each is delivered appropriately.

However, when a coach continues in one style when a transfer to the other might be more beneficial to the team, this typically contributes to miscommunication and ultimately a decrease in individual and team performance. Sometimes players may need more repetitive grounding in technique and strategy. This is not a time to let them be free-wheeling. Or, a team may

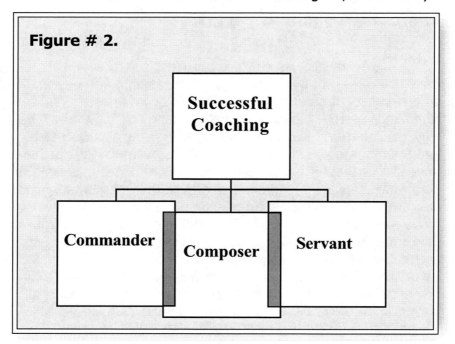

Figure # 2.

Successful Coaching

Commander

Composer

Servant

be over-coached with drills and plays. Some players have difficulty sorting out the "play book" in their heads, and subsequently become distracted in the game and make errors. When it is "my way or the highway" all the time, some players choose to take the path of least resistance, which leads to missed opportunities.

Balancing Coaching Styles

Alan McCoy says, "As a younger coach I was fiery to a fault and put too much emphasis on winning as an outcome independent of any other factors. I think young coaches often feel the need to be 'successful' in terms of wins before they will allow themselves to take a broader perspective on what they do. That was certainly the case for me. I remember working officials, pacing the sideline, using tactical fouls and sneaky plays. I also remember casting opponents as the enemy and thinking that portraying them as such was a good way to motivate the players in my charge. While my game intensity has lessened, my satisfaction with what I do has increased as I have matured as a coach. I think mentoring by veteran coaches can have a profound impact on young guys coming into coaching and can help them gain a healthy perspective in a fashion other than trial and error, which is how many of us learned."

Steve Koudelka, head men's coach at Lynchburg College, considers himself to be a 50 percent control, 25 percent servant, and 25 percent composer. He says, "I think each of these areas becomes more prevalent at different times. For example, I may be more of the control coach at practice and with off-field issues, but on game day, I may be more of the composer coach. To be successful you need to address the servant coach because empowering your players is very important."

The Commander/Controller

Some coaches will spend more time in the command/control environment with a young team, where systems may not be in place at that time. Reinforcing fundamentals at "all levels" is essential, however, and many coaches spend a lot of time "trying to convince" their players of this necessity. Dee Stephan's teams see about 75 percent of her coaching in the command/control arena. She feels women's lacrosse is a real strategy game and therefore, she wants her players to fully understand the tactics of the game, especially the ball control side of the game.

"The most important thing for a successful coach is to find the balance between strict discipline and ambition," says Bowen Holden. "I think that sometimes it's one extreme or the other. I think that when you can find that balance where you can establish the trust with your players through empathizing with them and through disciplining them they can learn far more, and they will learn right from wrong. I heard a quote the other day from a friend of mine's grandfather who was a headmaster. He coined the phrase 'choosing the hard right over the evil wrong,' and I think that is very true. I think that you need to have very strict discipline in order to establish that, and enable your players to learn those lessons that will carry them beyond the athletic field."

Dave Pietramala, head men's coach of 2005 national champion Johns Hopkins University, says he was very much a commander/controller in his first year at Hopkins. "It was a young team and time to change the culture of the program," he said. "However, last year's team had such a great group of seniors, I took on more of a servant leadership role."

On the other hand, Susie Ganzenmuller has observed coaches at women's high school and college levels who orchestrate their players' every move rather than letting their team think for themselves. Sometimes they fail and sometimes they succeed. This invites the controversial adage of "learning more from mistakes and failures than from successes."

The Servant Leader

Gordon Webb sees successful coaching as both a science and an art. He says, "The science is having an awareness of all factors that influence mastery and performance, and the art is having the coaching ability and sense when, where and how to apply these factors. When the teaching of techniques and tactics is blended with knowing how the player thinks and is motivated, the coach can get the most from his or her players."

Robert Greenleaf, the founder of the "servant leadership" movement, sees implications for lacrosse coaches. He says, "The servant-leader is servant first. It begins with the natural feeling that one wants to serve, to serve first. Then conscious choice brings one to aspire to lead. The difference manifests itself in the care taken by the servant to make sure that other people's highest priority needs are being served." He challenges adult mentors to ask and answer the important questions: "Do those served grow as persons? Do they, while being served, become healthier, wiser, freer, more autonomous, more likely themselves to become servants? And, what is the effect on the least privileged in society? Will they benefit, or at least, not be further deprived?"

If the answers to those questions lead to the conclusion that, indeed, our purpose is to serve (a conclusion that seems unavoidable), then we must be faithful to our service. We share the wonderful opportunity – and the privilege – of having a profound influence on others. Conor Gill, the 2004 MLL Most Valuable Player, a former All-American at Virginia, and now an assistant coach at his alma mater, says that the UVA coach's trust in him to be creative, to make mistakes, and eventually succeed took care of his needs and he responded accordingly. Sam Osherson claims that by way of their experience, good coaches bring a "shared wavelength" to the conversation with the player. By serving the player at this level, they truly live in the skin of the young person.

> *Service is the rent we pay for being. It is the very purpose of life and not something you do in your spare time.*
> —Marian Wright Edelman

Chris Paradis believes that less is more when it comes to over practicing the technical and tactical aspects of the game. Spend important time building relationships. She mentioned that the year they won the national championship was the year they practiced the least. She employed a variety of "team relationship" activities which helped to reduce distraction. Paradis cited a time the team hiked to a pond while talking about Amherst lacrosse and what it meant to each player. This is essential in order to build that trust that teams need in difficult times.

Dee Stephan admits to being a servant leader 20 percent of the time. "I think I try to serve the players' needs, I constantly think about how they are feeling and whether or not they feel taken care of," she describes. "I think with high school girls you can't help but use this style. They demand that they be taken care of. They speak their minds quite freely and they are unhappy when they just perform well." Success means to me that my players are having fun, learning and growing each game and supporting each other. I am proud that several players who have long since graduated still come home and check on Avon lacrosse to see the team play and reflect on their seasons."

Kate Dresher believes there needs to be a nice balance of the three styles at the girls' youth level. "If the drills and strategy are too complicated you will lose them," she says. "Fourth and fifth graders need more creativity. They are such spatial beings. Of course it is important to challenge them with a little bit of competition, but it is equally, if not more, important for coaches to provide frequent positive reinforcement. They must allow for all players to be included in all aspects of the team. Playing capture the flag is a common occurrence in the youth program."

The Composer/Conductor

Some successful coaches are more hands-off with their teams. In this case, they act more as a consultant to the team. At this stage, the players all know their responsibilities on the field and carry them out with great success, akin to gears meshing together. Dee Stephan wishes she could be more than a five percent composer/conductor, but she realizes the reality is that lacrosse isn't the main sport for many of her players, and learning their roles and responsibilities on the field is an on-going process.

Jack Light, head of the US Lacrosse South Florida chapter, believes there are many distractions for young people in South Florida and it is very important to provide more freedom of expression with youth players to keep them involved. He points to being a servant leader 40 percent of the time and composer/ conductor 50 percent of the time.

Roy Simmons, Jr. is considered the archetype of the composer/conductor coach. He believes that good coaches "have got to take their ego out of the game." Recently interviewed for a 2005 *Sports Illustrated* article on lacrosse, Simmons was also quoted in an 1983 SI article that had a sub-title reference to him - "I worked my medium as an artist creates a collage." As a coach, his teams are his collages.

The Artist and His Collage

I have seen in many high schools where there is a command-control — my way or the highway coaching mentality. You don't take a thoroughbred horse and bring him to a Kentucky Derby and, you, as a jockey, are told to hold him back and make him run the way you want him to run. You let him go. I felt that way. Richie Moran, at Cornell, used to tease me, "When I used to scout you prior to playing you in a couple of weeks, I tried to figure out your offense. I'd look at it like a Chinese fire-drill." That was a great insult and I think he meant it that way too.

We were typically pretty unpredictable, and there were many times when I felt that I didn't have as good a team. I would let the kids have a little bit more leeway, let them run and gun. Yeah, we will probably give up some goals and will be caught flat-footed on a fast break now and then, but as we spread it and go to the cage, everybody has license. We don't have FOGO's and shooters. We all are involved in the program. With good talent, I let the kids run free and we would be a little bit unpredictable.

I try to understand my players, as I am a teacher first, on and off the field. I want to be accessible. I want them to come to me with a problem and to level with me. Maybe they can't with their mother and father. Maybe they can't with their roommates or teammates. I want to be sure that they know there is no reprisal that they would be moved from first to second midfield because they told me something. I want them to know that. I want them to respect me. If they do respect me, I have better control of the team as opposed to some coaches that are "hellfire and

continued on next page...

...continued from previous page

brimstone." I can remember when we played Brown when Dom Starsia was coaching. I consider him a friend and a real gentleman. I have always admired Dom. He wasn't as successful against Syracuse when he was at Brown then he went to Virginia. Around his third year at Virginia, he had a great team, a lot of talent. But he didn't want to play UVA lacrosse – they didn't have that white oxford shirt underneath their jersey. Instead, he let them go, which was bad for us. He let their imagination and fantasy go and they beat us pretty good. After the game, as we do, shake hands and he looked at me and said, "You know Roy, I beat you at your game." I said, what are you talking about – you beat me at my game. You just beat me soundly, you have got a great team, Dom. He said, "No, I beat you at your game. I looked at your offense and I looked at your defense and I looked at the way that you treat these kids, and I decided that it was time that we would play Syracuse style." Just like Syracuse basketball, you get a fast break, and everybody has license to initiate. I just believe if you recruit thorough-breds, you have got to let them go.

You got to let the kids prove to one another, who they are and what they got and why they deserve to play and why the coaches let them do what they do – then everything else falls in place.

—*Roy Simmons Jr., Former Men's Head Coach, Syracuse University*

4

The Right Questions — As a coach, how do you balance your roles as a Commander/Controller, Servant Leader and Composer/Conductor? Taking each of the three styles into consideration, what percentage would you ideally assign to each approach? What percentage would you assign in reality to your coaching styles?

The Roles and Responsibilities of Officiating

The qualities of a successful official are somewhat different. Most importantly a good official must be able to remove himself or herself from the emotion of the game. An official must be able to remain consistent throughout a contest and establish a clear set of acceptable practices. He or she must be able to feel the flow of the game and adjust accordingly. Someone once said that the best official in any contest is one that you don't even notice. There is a great deal of truth to that statement. The contest is supposed to be about the players and coaches going head to head and in an ideal situation, those individuals decide the outcome. For officials to be successful, they need to oversee the rules of the contest, but never interfere with the outcome of the game. It is also important to enjoy being there – you can tell when an official is preoccupied and doesn't care.

The Responsibilities of Lacrosse Officiating

Successful officials are physically fit and arrive professionally dressed and on time for every game. We must be firm but friendly in our interactions with players. We must give our full effort for every game, at every level of the game. Integrity and teamwork are the key to success! Call only what you see, don't make up calls or call something that you think will happen. Know the rules and the current rules interpretations, but umpire the game. Respect all participants. Attend coach and umpire training clinics. Watch video tapes. Be human, have fun and love what you do. Earn the respect of players, coaches and other officials, while also respecting yourself and your responsibilities.

—*Susie Ganzenmuller, 2005 National Lacrosse Hall of Fame Inductee*

Good officials have the desire and ability to adapt to the changes in the culture and rules of the game. Susie Ganzenmuller states, "To stay current with any game, officials have to study game tapes and attend coaching and officiating workshops to learn what the players are being taught. Rules books annually get thicker and thicker as coaches learn to manipulate rules." She adds, "One must learn to umpire the game and not just the rules. It takes years to learn when and when not to hold the whistle. Mere possession of the ball is not necessarily an advantage. A player must have a quality possession with the opportunity to be able to do something good with the ball. It takes a long time for officials to develop the courage to give cards and to know how to effectively use cards to control a game in the event that one team is taking advantage of the rules."

Top officials develop their common sense so that they can think quickly and deal with situations that are not specifically addressed in the rules. Experience gives an official the courage to broaden their off-ball vision to better see the big picture.

"Officially" Experienced

When I was young I was more authoritative. As I have grown in stature and confidence, I get my point across with less enthusiasm. I am still as stern when I need to be. In a Division III College game last season, I stopped my count when a player almost went out of bounds, with the opposing coach screaming for 10 seconds. At the same time, the other coach was screaming for a timeout. The other official granted the timeout. The three officials had a conference and I then went over and explained I screwed up. I had played college ball against one of the other coaches, who then said, "OK, Jimmy." Defusing the situation with my admission allowed for everyone to get back into the game.

—*Jimmy Tighe, Men's Lacrosse Official, New England Lacrosse Hall of Fame Inductee*

The Challenges of Officiating

"As an official gets older and slower, she must anticipate where the ball will go next so that she has the opportunity to move and be in the right position to make accurate calls," says Ganzenmuller. Experienced officials also develop "long" eyes. It takes many years to develop officiating wisdom, and by that time, your physical ability to keep up with play begins to wane. The committed women's official consistently abides by the following credo: "While I may not like a new rule or like the way a rule is interpreted, I must be true to the game and call rules according to how the rules committee and rules interpreter directs us to do so."

With societal changes paralleling the growth of the women's game, more women now compete with men for the more high-powered jobs as lawyers, doctors and as leaders in business and technology. It seems more difficult for women to juggle their families and jobs to make time for coaching and officiating. Since women are unable or are choosing not to give back to the game, women are partly responsible for the recent increase in the ratio of male to female coaches and officials. In the past more women were teachers, service volunteers and homemakers which may have afforded them greater opportunity and available free time to coach and umpire.

Matt Palumb believes that "less is more" when it comes to calling a good game. By being in great condition and being able to be in the right place at the right time, the official then gets a better look at the play. He says, "Don't blow the whistle just to blow it."

John Hill laments that he has observed an increase in youth and high school players who are imitating their coaches on the field. "If the coach is a screamer, the players will feel they can do the same things," he says. "On the other hand, if the coach is very professional and considerate, the players usually are the same. College players usually find their own level and will behave differently in different situations. They realize the intensity of the game, and police themselves most of the time." Hill admits in his years of officiating that, "A player of great character will become a better player because, if all things are equal, then the player with the greater character (heart) will come out on top."

When new lacrosse programs first begin, the need for and development of a qualified officials' pool is often an afterthought. Officials' training programs sometimes begin as many as two years after area coaches and players are exposed to the game. There can be pressure to cover games and assign rookies to officiate high-level games before they are ready to handle that level of play. Many rookies become frustrated and quit. Ganzenmuller is cautious about this matter. She is also concerned about the education of the male coaches and male officials entering the women's game. This number outpaces former female players who stay involved with the game to coach or officiate.

"A lot of male coaches and officials come to the women's game from the men's game. Some outstanding players from the men's game, such as Gary Gait, assistant coach of the women's team at Maryland during its seven-year run as the NCAA Division I champion, have made very positive contributions to the women's game. Gary respected our game, but too many men do not buy into the women's game and its rules and their involvement is effectively changing how the women's game is played. Traditionally, women's lacrosse is based upon players' speed and finesse rather than deliberate body-to-body and stick-to-body contact. Women are very concerned that our game is becoming more similar to the men's game," says Ganzenmuller.

Two prevailing thoughts that many good officials are concerned about are win at all cost and anything is legal until you get caught, the decrease in respect for officials. As mentioned earlier, the coaches and the officials become the "adults" in charge of the game. Keeping the line of communication between coaches and officials open will help to decrease some of the concerns stated above. However, this is not an easy task. Additionally, when officials learn more about a fellow official's background, this makes the game better, because the officials tend to better understand that person's personal "quirks" and how they may need to adjust to make the game together go more smoothly.

One Game – One Goal

Rob Pfeiffer focused on officiating after his coaching years at Middlebury and Colby. He remembers, "I was lucky enough to be officiating on a crew at UMass. Both teams were ranked in the top 10 at the time and they were also dedicating Garber Field.

There was a huge contrast in style with both coaches. When we went onto the field to check the goals the visiting team coach made some nasty remark and wouldn't say hello while he was warming up the goalie. He then goes on the point out that goal is too short. So while he is shooting, I am measuring the height. Sure thing – it was 71 inches. He starts yapping in a really nasty tone, "What are you gong to do about?

continued on next page...

...continued from previous page

We are not going to play this way. We will walk off the field." I tell him, "I am sure the grounds crew can handle this, no problem, we can get somebody to come over there." So we get the grounds crew to resolve the situation. However, I noticed that throughout the game he had coaches timing us, four seconds and 10 seconds. For any rule that had a time component to it, his assistant coaches had a stop watch on it – continually yelling at us from the sidelines letting us know, 'That was nine seconds! That was 4.35 seconds!' If this is the way it is going to be, then this is crazy. So the game ended up in a fight, a brawl between both teams. I had to pull one of the officials out from under the two teams. The tone of it was that the parents were echoing the coaches and then the players got into it. You could see it just all go downhill. That is the fear—you have Garbs and Teddy doing it the way you expect it to be and this other business going on. It's going to come back around on you, you know. To believe that someone can't say, "Hello, nice to see you today. I am a little concerned about the team goal: could you check it for me?" I don't respond very well to the former thing, no matter what I have on my shoes. It raises my hackles. Well, the opposing team ended up losing the game. It wasn't because of the yellow flags. They probably didn't have that many penalties anyway. But their players were so distracted by this imaginary game of parent/coaches versus the officials. If the coaches, officials and parents don't act like adults the 30 or 50 or however many kids you have are going to lose the benefits of an opportunity to learn something that afternoon. All the adults – coaches, officials and parents – ought to be on the same page.

—Rob Pfeiffer, Men's Former Official & Coach,
　Middlebury College

4

The Right Question — How do you as a player, coach, official, parent or administer work in concert with officials so that there are the least distractions for the players?

SECTION 3

Sportsmanship and Character Development

Chapter 5

Character Comes Alive

I am not convinced that lacrosse or other sports form char-
acter, but I am convinced that those players and
coaches with certain character traits are more likely
to succeed in lacrosse than those who do not possess
the following traits – a passion for excellence, a
great work ethic, a total understanding and appre-
ciation for the game.

—Jim Wilson, Head Boys' Coach, Loomis-Chaffee
School, CT

To truly commit to honoring the game of lacrosse, all participants must know what good character looks like when it comes alive on the field and how to celebrate it, especially for players in their youth. Sportsmanship is about developing positive habits so they become second nature. It is about behavior, and for some, about learning to change behavior. Just as strong stick work means countless hours on the wall, positive habits only happen when players, coaches, officials, administrators and spectators make serious and enduring efforts to act within the spirit of the game.

Lacrosse coaches and parents of players are, by nature, character educators. When there is common ground among adult participants, the program sends a more consistent message to the athletes. We all possess a character—whether it be ill- or well-formed. This chapter examines the foundation of good character and defines those core values that support the establishment of common ground of all lacrosse teams and programs. This is a critical element of this book, just as it is a critical element for the game of lacrosse.

Good character is not only observed in sportsmanlike behavior. It is embedded in the roots that are displayed in the perseverance of mastering stick fundamentals and developing a keen sense of game flow. This is no easy task. It takes diligent practice over time to develop these dispositions through rehearsal and reinforcement. This is about mastering a craft.

Kevin Hicks says that "the act of developing good character is a process of finding and then accepting the presence of the good, whatever it is. [It is] encouraging players, coaches, officials and parents to find it, embrace [it] and then accept and defend it, ideally. And acquiring good habits is not just ritual. It more often than not involves a human relationship. Organized activity becomes a vehicle by which those relationships can be performed, acted out and explored. Part of it, too, is the whole idea of being able, once you have the sense of good in your life, to act out appropriate behaviors on the lacrosse field. It allows you to tell the truth about yourself a little bit more. To live without alibi. To be willing to take your lumps. In really simple terms, it means knowing that whatever penalty you pay for doing whatever you've done is going to be somehow less an issue than working to avoid that punishment. And that is the goal — to live and play the game as simply as possible and without all the emotional apparatus that you think you need to have in lacrosse and, ultimately, in your daily life."

There is a strong relationship between character and performance. Most coaches are in the business of human performance. This can't be ignored. However, many coaches separate the character piece from the actual strategy and task on the field. In actuality, the two are vitally interconnected. Most people involved in lacrosse strive to win. Regardless of winning or losing, a person's character should remain the same. Despite the logical link between character and performance, many coaches continue to consider the myth that paying too much attention to the player's character will soften their focus on performance. It is interesting that 85 percent of the respondents in the US Lacrosse survey claimed that there ought to be a balance between an emphasis on character development and winning. In retrospect, character development and winning are not mutually exclusive.

If properly organized, prepared for, and taught, lacrosse offers athletes and coaches a unique opportunity for cooperation, growth and development. Certainly at the high school level, coaches have an opportunity to bring student athletes and a community together. 'Community' in this case is really a complex of communities. For example, at the high school level there is the school community, but on a larger scale, there is the town full of parents, siblings, alums and other curious parties invested in the game. The lacrosse community also is invested in every team and opponent. Many players and coaches pick up the paper the day after game day or check on a web site for scores and read about who made the big plays in the next town over.

Community and character are linked because the careful coach ensures that his or her players understand they are playing (and practicing) for something larger than just their own satisfaction. "We try to link community and character in a few ways," says John Pirani. "One way is that we believe in taking road trips to schools that are not in our league or even out of state. In that way, we try to link the lacrosse community across distances. Doing so broadens our local community and exposes it to a broader lacrosse community. On a local level, our high school players coach youth teams as a part of our effort to perform community service and give back to lacrosse and the town. The youth players our seniors coach are our ball boys on game days. As a result, our players play in front of boys they coach. This is a wonderful opportunity for our players to be role models at a relatively young age and come to understand how important and influential they are in the lives of younger boys.

On a team level, we ought to work diligently to ensure that players understand the need to accept personal responsibility for their performances. At the same time, the goal of team success is constantly at the forefront. We have a policy that no player is allowed to say, 'My bad' in the event of a misstep on their part. In lacrosse, as in many other sports, an individual's success or failure has team implications. 'My bad' merely exonerates the individual, but what about the team? We make the assumption that everyone on the field is trying as hard as they can, so 'my bad' means nothing. In stadiums when we play a night game and they introduce the team one at a time, we clap but stay together. On days when one player messes up, the whole team runs. Is the goalie the only player that gives up a goal, or is a goal a result of seven defenders not effectively defending a shot opportunity? We hold paramount the idea that every individual on the team has a role, and that role contributes to the whole team effort."

Properly communicated, team goals always transcend the accomplishments or failures of individuals. "I think coaches who try to develop character in a heavy-handed manner miss the point," says Pirani. Character is not developed in young men by running sprints until the team is dizzy. Character is working with the whole student-athlete and helping him or her find his place in the team and world. Character is extrinsically encouraged and intrinsically driven. Lacrosse presents a wonderful opportunity to emphasize and revisit the many ways young men can come together and achieve more as a whole than they can as individuals. As coaches, we have a great opportunity to provide the best environment possible for players to develop for themselves and with their teammates. In times when society seems to gratify a "me first" approach to the world, lacrosse presents an opportunity to achieve as a cooperative group seeking a singular goal. The coaching challenge is to articulate the goal and to ensure that team comes first and individuals prosper only if they contribute to the whole. For a healthy environment, these expectations ought to be made clear to the stakeholders involved.

However, reaching consensus on these matters is not always easy. Consequently, it is important that all concerned forge an agreement on the behaviors that are expected on and off the field of play, and a common language that defines the "right" actions. When adults use words such as connection, leadership, trust, respect, spirit, and commitment to youth, the meaning must be associated with the actions. They ought to be certain that the players understand the meaning and intention behind these words. When we give clear and consistent age-appropriate messages to the athletes in our care, there is a greater likelihood that they will be inspired to act in an acceptable manner.

For some coaches, making the commitment to develop and maintain a character-based lacrosse program is a difficult challenge. Although most coaches have good intentions and truly believe that "character matters" in the lacrosse experience, such intentions and beliefs may not be enough. They must also know what virtue looks like when it comes alive on the field. They must understand that virtue is about developing habits so they become second nature. Just like learning wall ball, repetition of the behavior eventually yields a habit.

As there are no "just add water" methods for a player to develop strong fundamental stickwork or smooth and flowing team concepts, change in behavior can only happen when people make serious and enduring efforts. Jeff Beedy's book, *Sports Plus*, addresses the importance of understanding the different ways that people learn. Basing his insights on learning theory, Beedy emphasizes three activities that help bring virtue to life in sports: modeling, dialogue and consequences. To apply this theory, we need only ask a series of pointed questions. If, for example, we believe a lacrosse program is about trust and fairness, we can ask:

- What do trust and fairness look like when they are modeled by coaches and players? How does this behavior look in the performance of individual players and the collective team?
- What are the characteristics of dialogue or conversation that go on between coaches and players, and between the players themselves, that indicates a level of trust?
- What are the consequences for a team or individual player when a coach, player or parent has broken trust with reference?

Better yet, let's reframe that last question so that it has a positive spin: What are the consequences for a team or player when all involved consistently trust each other? The answer is simple – greater enjoyment and satisfaction, and, in most cases, improved performance. We learn by knowing, by valuing, and by acting. There is no substitute for developing and reinforcing the "second nature habits" of good character.

Doing Right by the Game

When I was interviewed by the University of Virginia thirteen years ago, they asked me to describe myself. I said that I didn't really know how to do that, but I can promise you that I will be honest and I work really hard. People who get to this level all have a sufficient knowledge of the game at a strategic level. Some of us are better at it than others. However, you have to be willing to work hard. You have to have great passion and enthusiasm for it. You always talk about doing it right – doing it with a sense of honesty, because at the end of the day, if you are in it for the long haul, that is how you are going to build a foundation that actually lasts. You may win a game or two and win a recruit or two in any particular situation by taking some shortcuts. But, I have been in this long enough to appreciate that we have done it the right way, and I am not looking over my shoulder about something I said or something I did. And there are times in your life, in this game, in coaching when you are faced with making those kinds of decisions. It is awfully hard to resist the temptation –but in the long run, I try to live by that credo.

—Dom Starsia, Head Men's Coach, University of VA

Susie Ganzenmuller has observed that the women's game has grown so quickly that there are many collegiate coaches who, once they've graduated from college, immediately land high-profile coaching jobs. They never had the opportunity to learn the head coaching job by first being an assistant coach. Being fresh out of college, there may not be enough appropriate difference between the maturity level of these young coaches and their players. At high school play days attended by college coaches for recruiting purposes, some players are more concerned with showing off their individual skills rather than showcasing themselves as part of a great team. "I see more deliberate breakdown/professional fouls than in the past" she says. "The prevailing societal ethic 'nothing is illegal until one gets caught', applies to how we play games as well. Too many female coaches curse to motivate their players. From the sidelines, coaches now orchestrate their players' every move rather than letting their team think for themselves; some fail and some succeed. In my life, I have learned way more from my mistakes and failures than from my successes."

Character Cornerstones

We have cornerstones that are the most important values of the Haverford lacrosse program. They come down to four categories – enthusiasm, effort, judgment and competitive drive.

We want to have a work ethic, and we actually give out an award called the "hard hat" which is for the hardest working guy on the team – each week. The enthusiasm piece is covered by making sure that lacrosse is fun. This is college lacrosse at the D3 level – I try to be appreciative of the difference, although it's minuscule. We do the same stuff as D1, but the level of athlete is a step below and we are not allowed to be with them in an organized fashion between the end of fall lacrosse and the beginning of the spring season. Everything we do – the practices, are the same. We want to make it fun! Nobody is here because they have to be here. All the players and coaches are here because they love lacrosse.

Judgment is more about making the decisions – being smart. I got a lot of this from reading Dean Smith's book – play hard, play smart, play together and have fun. It's really the same four things in slightly different variations, though. We try to include things on and off the field and in the classroom. We make it a point for our guys to care about their schoolwork and to be responsible. And the competitive drive is something that you have to be about more than talk about. We take a lot of pride in performance and results, and make a lot of our drills competitive.

—Mike Murphy, Head Men's Coach, Haverford College

There are coaches who sign on a class of freshman players and each is outstanding in her own right. The team does not have the winning record that one would expect- why? It seems that some coaches over-train their players as too many are hurt and on the sidelines. "It is easy to recognize coaches who play favorites and to see tension that creates among other players on a team," says Susie Ganzenmuller. "The joy is gone from the team. When I have made an unpopular call, I have had a coach yell, 'Susie, you are killing us.' While I would never re-spond, I think to myself, 'I'm not killing you, your player is killing you.' Your player is totally undisciplined, out of control and a selfish showboat. I see too many players who are burned out when they graduate from college and walk away from the game forever." This phenomenon is supported by Frank Deford, the well-known *Sports Illustrated* writer: "Perhaps what has happened in sports suggests primarily that we have less respect for author-ity," he says. "Players don't seem to see the officials as custodi-ans of the game so much as obstacles to work around, to fool."

"Officially" Human

Some coaches and spectators have made it their right to publicly criticize and demean officials. For the most part, players do not speak back to me. I think they know that I respect them and their athletic abilities even though I sometimes have to step in to facilitate fair and safe play. The game is not about me, it is about the athletes, and I am in awe of their stick work, speed and grace on the field. They see me trying my best and being willing to listen and quickly answer questions when asked. Over the years, I have also learned to quickly correct mistakes during a game, and I think this has made me seem more human and earned me added respect as an official.

— *Susie Ganzenmuller, Women's Official, 2005*
National Lacrosse Hall of Fame Inductee

Role Modeling Good Character

Parents are the major character educators of their children, whether they be an U11 youth player, or post-collegiate club player. Young people are highly influenced by adult behavior and also adult hypocrisy – "Do as I say, not as I do?"

Gene Zanella supports the reality that many parents have instilled positive moral values in their children who have already developed strong character traits by the time they reach high school. As high school coaches, we spend so much time with our players, we should reinforce what they have been taught with every action we take. Hard work, commitment and dedication will be mirrored by our athletes; as will cheating, cutting corners, swearing, or any negative attributes if the athlete has not developed his or her true character. High school students are struggling to develop their own character identity and are looking for role models wherever they can be found. "The coach sets the tone for the character of the team and helps keep it on course, especially for younger players. The coach must model the character she expects from her players," says Missy Foote.

Youth coaches have similar responsibilities as positive role models; however the time of contact with athletes is much less. High school coaches will spend 15 to 20 hours per week with an athlete while youth coaches will spend five to eight hours a week with the athlete. The opportunity for a youth coach to influence an athlete's character can be magnified for the athlete who falls in love with the game of lacrosse because he or she will follow the example set by the coach.

"Consistency in your lifestyle will result in better performance – in every aspect," says Jack Piatelli, who works for Warrior and is a former college and professional indoor player. On the other side, he claims that youth and high school players are negatively influenced by the inconsistency of coaches who lack experience.

One of the questions on the US Lacrosse survey was, "Which coaches, players, administrators, or officials do you consider to be role models in lacrosse and why?" The 805 responses were, in most cases, remarkably consistent regarding the core values of lacrosse: connection, leadership, respect, spirit, tradition, trust and youth. These values are embedded in comments such as "selfless in their motivation to work with people," "she really cares about her players," "their ideas on teamwork, discipline and on-the-field manners have shaped me as a lacrosse player and as a person in general," and "for his ability to connect with people." One respondent offered: "The role model is 'Gags' (John Gagliardi), because he's amazing and he plays old school – how lax is supposed to be played." Or another about Maureen O'Shea – "she provides total involvement, no nonsense positive fundamental instruction, sportsmanship and positive reinforcement."

The US Lacrosse survey also asked members if they considered U.S. team athletes and staff to be role models. Eighty-three percent of the respondents either agreed or strongly agreed with the statement. The responses included comments on what the sample thought the ideal role should be:

- "Any time you are chosen to represent a group because of your talents, you have a responsibility to portray a positive example, whether you want to or not."
- "For the youth of lacrosse, the U.S. team can bring so much needed excitement and publicity."
- "I think they have young player's attentions and are looked at as role models. I am not certain they see themselves as such and not certain all players conduct themselves as role models. I have seen some that do."
- "They need to be. I feel it's their obligation because our youth needs it these days."
- "These athletes have been given a privilege to play and travel around the world."

The reality for some respondents includes:

- "While they are role models, I'm not sure they always deliver the best message to the youth of the sport— particularly through the treatment of officials."
- "We should find role models within and from the U.S.

teams. Athletes are not considered role models just by the plain fact that a player is on a US Team. They are not automatic role models."

- "Kids look up to these athletes and staff and they have a responsibility to be role models and to represent the game and the USA honorably."
- "Through their touring and clinics, they act as role models teaching kids."

If you were to ask the majority of Jim Wilson's former players at Loomis-Chaffee, they can attest to the fact that everything he says and recognizes revolves around the following traits: a passion for excellence, work ethic, a total understanding and appreciation for the game, self-discipline, a desire to be independent, and the ability to attend to details and postpone gratification. Most important to Wilson is for his players to under-stand that if one trains hard (and well) and learns the basics, and is willing to work as part of a larger whole – then good things will happen. This is all about process, not outcome. Wilson empha-sizes, "I cannot control the outcome in a lacrosse game or in life, but I can control what I do every day to prepare and what I do every day to work with my teammates. I think this is the biggest lesson for life – work hard at what you can control and the results will take care of themselves. I want to win, but I can go to bed each night, content, if I know I HAVE done everything possible to help my players prepare. At Loomis Chaffee we rarely talk about outcomes. We talk a lot about process, about self-control and about accountability. The goal is not to control or make the kids obedient to some authority. The goal is for them to learn to be independent and self-reliant people – and lacrosse is a vehicle for helping them do this."

Shaun Stanton agrees with Wilson's tenets. "Players are motivated by coaches to play well. Players strive to meet the expectations of the coaches and play well. In doing so, they have formed part of their character," he says.

States of Character

Although the ancient Greek philosopher Aristotle never played the game, his maxims are demonstrated on the lacrosse field today. Steve Tigner, a professor at Boston University, illustrates the classical Greek philosopher's States of Character as: acting brutishly; acting with self-indulgence; acting with weakness of will; acting with strength of will; acting with character excellence; and acting with a superhuman, saintly virtue. Brutish actions are typically reserved for a pre-human state, although we may see this occasionally in some "moral lepers." On the opposite end, there are few people who are saintly and possess heroic virtue. This is typically reserved for acts of great courage and sacrifice above and beyond the call of duty (See Figure 3 that follows).

However, what we observe more on and off the lacrosse field are the middle four states. A "defective" character is observed in coaches, players, parents or fans who act self-indulgently. For example, a player is aggressively fouled by a member of the opposing team. Unfortunately, the official's angle didn't see the direct point of the infraction. The fouled player is incensed and gets up off the ground and gets right in the officials face, precipitating an unsportsmanlike call, be it a card (women's game) or three-minute unreleasable call (men's game).

Weakness of will or caving into temptation, is the next step up in the character "food chain." The player, coach or parent who has difficulties managing his or her behavior, however, may know intellectually what they should do and how they should respond. They have the best intentions, but are still lured into the wrong behavior. The person knows they shouldn't respond to the controversial non-call, but does so with less impact than of self-indulgence, but enough to receive a penalty. Another example is players who have practiced their fundamentals to earn the fruits of good stick, such as the boy who continues to take side-arm shots that go in every direction but the goal. Without deliberate rehearsal of the skill, the player is "wishing" rather than "willing" to make the skill a reality.

Although a player, coach or parent may still have the desire to act in this way, they are no longer controlled by the desire, and establish a strength of will, or mastering of temptation. The impulse is to respond to the official, but the person chooses to act under control. Mastering temptation takes effort. It is not easy and can be very frustrating. So, the player immediately gets off the ground and stays with the play, possibly fuming inside about the non-call, but still physically present in the game.

Through diligent practice and rehearsal, the stakeholder is no longer tempted to act out in such a situation. This person performs right actions as a matter of habit – an attitude influenced by balancing precise thought about short- and long-term consequences. With the above scenario, a person of character excellence, or moderation, is nonplused by the non-call, but knows that it is part of the game and part of being human.

When individual players and collective teams "go with the flow," they are not compromised by the little distractions. Another example of character excellence was witnessed in one of our managers at Culver. As the official timekeeper, he was counting down the last seconds of a home team penalty. The player in the box left early and Scott immediately blew the horn to gain the official's attention. Although he had friends on the home team, he realized his responsibility to uphold the rules of the game. The official sent the player back into the box again, much to the chagrin and subtle comments of disdain to Scott: "Why would you do that to one of our players?" Scott Evans was not bothered by the comments, and kept his focus on "what mattered most." I was very proud of his behavior as he protected the "truth" and the integrity of the game that day.

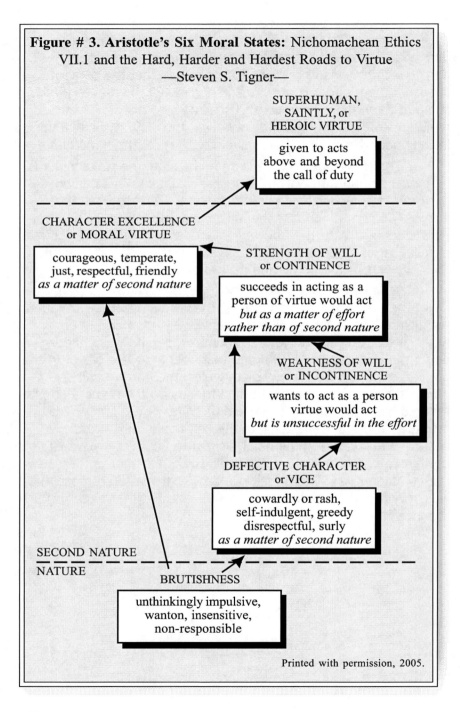

Figure # 3. Aristotle's Six Moral States: Nichomachean Ethics VII.1 and the Hard, Harder and Hardest Roads to Virtue
—Steven S. Tigner—

SUPERHUMAN,
SAINTLY, or
HEROIC VIRTUE

given to acts
above and beyond
the call of duty

CHARACTER EXCELLENCE
or MORAL VIRTUE

courageous, temperate,
just, respectful, friendly
as a matter of second nature

STRENGTH OF WILL
or CONTINENCE

succeeds in acting as a
person of virtue would act
*but as a matter of effort
rather than of second nature*

WEAKNESS OF WILL
or INCONTINENCE

wants to act as a person
virtue would act
but is unsuccessful in the effort

DEFECTIVE CHARACTER
or VICE

cowardly or rash,
self-indulgent, greedy
disrespectful, surly
as a matter of second nature

SECOND NATURE
NATURE

BRUTISHNESS

unthinkingly impulsive,
wanton, insensitive,
non-responsible

Printed with permission, 2005.

The Stupid Point

When lacrosse participants have developed a good character, they have formed enduring habits of the head, heart and hand. They know what is right and continually practice right action. So when an ethical dilemma arises, a coach, athlete, parent or official who has a well-formed character has less difficulty making the proper behavior choice. Knowing, valuing and acting on the "good" prevents the situation from becoming a problem. However, there are moments when lacrosse participants have known and valued the good, but have acted in a very different way. Ken Dryden, a member of the Canadian House of Commons and former professional hockey great, has always been an advocate for the decrease of violence that many associate with hockey. He claims that every person has a "stupid point." It basically means that most participants know better, but the heat of the moment causes them to break down and act as if they had never been exposed to good in their lives. We all make mistakes. However, a well-formed character helps limit these sojourns to the dark side.

Dryden was called to investigate and make sense of a Canadian college hockey game gone ugly in 1996 – a referee was assaulted while players from both teams were involved in a brief, yet disturbing melee. "As the temperature rises," Dryden explained, "the distance between out of control *good*, and out of control *bad* is tiny. Our own personal 'stupid point' is always perilously near. Something happens and we trip over the edge." However, a well-formed character decreases the odds of a person acting in such a brutish way. For example, I spoke with an assistant high school lacrosse coach who regularly had to restrain the team's head coach – a person who tended to "lose it" by the third quarter of each game. Although the head coach was consistent in reaching the stupid point, the players on the field and sideline had to witness behavior that is inconsistent with how coaches ought to act. This mixed message can be distracting from moment-to-moment concentration on the field. Athletes would never get away with behavior like that. On the other hand, some players at the higher levels of lacrosse are so used to their coaches "going nuts," that they easily dismiss the behavior and their play is not negatively influenced. They "selectively attend" to the coaches behavior.

Some coaches, players and parents occasionally dismiss inappropriate adult or adolescent behavior in the manner that many people used to gloss over the behavior of a drunken person—saying for example, "they aren't usually like that." The equivalent to this on the lacrosse field is to say something to the effect of, "Oh, they got caught up in the moment – the fever pitch of the game brought them there. They normally don't act this way." We are witnessing more "stupid point" behavior these days. We intellectually know that this behavior doesn't make the game better.

Sportsmanship, Gamesmanship and Lacrosse

> *Where once we valued sportsmanship, now we prize what we have come to call "gamesmanship." But I think values have changed. Hey, we've always wanted to win. It's just that now we're much more accepting—forgiving, even—about the means to victory. And, as is so often the case with our sports, this pretty much reflects the attitude we possess about other elements of our whole broad society."*
>
> —Frank Deford, *Gamesmanship vs Sportsmanship*

The actions of sportsmanship and gamesmanship differ in the minds of different lacrosse participants. The *American Heritage Dictionary* has very appropriate definitions of sportsmanship and gamesmanship:

sports·man·ship [spôrts·mən-shĭp', spôrts'-]
n.

1. The fact or practice of participating in sports or a sport.
2. Conduct and attitude considered as befitting participants in sports, especially fair play, courtesy, striving spirit, and grace in losing.

games·man·ship [gā́mz·mən-shĭp']
n.

1. The art or practice of using tactical maneuvers to further one's aims or better one's position.

2. The use in a sport or game of aggressive, often dubious tactics, such as psychological intimidation or disruption of concentration, to gain an advantage over one's opponent.

Gaining an edge includes coaches riding officials to eventually get calls in their favor; stick-doctoring (more so in the men's game); and subtle face-off cheating. "Edge has become a much more important word in our language. Everybody is looking for an edge," says Frank Deford.

Dave Antol, an official, youth lacrosse coach, PCA facilitator and parent of two Division I men's goalies, was involved in a very interesting discussion with other officials regarding the use of gamesmanship. The discussion came about after a coach had named a play called "flag down." Every time he called the play from the sidelines, the other team would become distracted expecting an ensuing penalty. For that nanosecond there was a loss of concentration, and the "flag down" team would take advantage. The officials decided that the intention behind the call was deceitful and, therefore, ruled that the coach not be allowed to make reference to the terminology in this situation.

Another interesting development in the game, on the men's side is the subtle "warding off" done in the "swim move," a type of dodge where the ball handler brings the stick high above his head and swooshes it down, while at the same time (and not all players do this) uses the free hand and elbow to push off the defender. While the official may focus the movement of the stick above the head, the "hidden" hand is in covert action pushing the defender away. On the women's side, some defending players are now being coached to enter shooting space with great regularity, to distract the offensive shooter. The penalty is still called, but it prevents the game from being played the way it should be played. This really marginalizes a good offensive player.

Michael Josephson, the founder of the Josephson Institute for Ethics, says, "gamesmanship approaches adopt the values of the marketplace, encouraging and sanctioning clever and effective ways of bending, evading and breaking the rules in order to gain a competitive advantage. This is considered part of the game." He also claims that "gamesmanship coaches and athletes are pragmatists, believing that ethical standards are determined by practical consideration of what works, rather than principles of what's right. One of the serious problems with gamesmanship is that there are no criteria for drawing a line between what is acceptable and what is not."

5

The Right Question — What, if any, are some acts of gamesmanship that you, your team and opponents currently employ? Are they "ethical"? If so, why? If not, why not?

Views, Values and Virtues

It is the belief of many lacrosse enthusiasts that virtuous behavior serves as a foundation for good action in sport. However, people's views and values are not necessarily based on virtue. Highly charged views (based on self-interest and seen in many lacrosse chat rooms) and questionable values (based on individual thoughts and feelings) can sometimes be disguised as virtuous behavior. Therefore, it is important to understand the differences between views, values and virtues through a framework developed by leading character educators, Kevin Ryan and Karen Bohlin.

Note the differences in the following scenarios as compared to views and values. The importance of thoughtful reflection on virtue as a foundation is the prime theme in this discussion. Therefore, if you declare that you run a character-based team program, and your actions are based on views and values without regard to virtue, then your means and your ends are not in synch. When this happens, it is a red flag to make sure that the core virtues of the program are known, valued, and acted upon consistently.

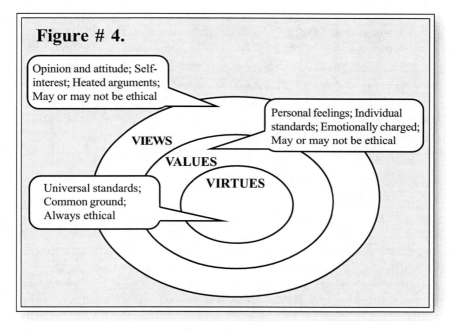

Figure # 4.

Opinion and attitude; Self-interest; Heated arguments; May or may not be ethical

Personal feelings; Individual standards; Emotionally charged; May or may not be ethical

VIEWS

VALUES

VIRTUES

Universal standards; Common ground; Always ethical

Views

Many adult sport participants have strong opinions about sport. It would be safe to say that most people who step onto the playing field or sit in the stands – coach, athlete, parent, or official—regard the experience from their own "private universe". Controversies among sport stakeholders are driven by self-interest and there is a wide range of compelling arguments about the social issues involved in sport. It is common to have many points of view about any given issue. What some people believe to be most important about sports participation may differ and be in conflict with one another.

VIEWS are beliefs and opinions that come from an intellectual standpoint. They do not necessarily

transmit to behavior. Views may or may not be moral/ethical.

Kevin Ryan and Karen Bohlin, in *Building Character in Schools,* state that "there is nothing wrong with generating controversy in the careful pursuit of the truth. Controversy can prompt reflection, thought and insight—but it can also provoke anger, resentment and a contentious spirit that spills out of control." At the end of these typically active conversations, parties go their separate ways with no healthy resolution to the situation. Ryan and Bohlin claim, "Some subjects end up generating more heat than light." This behavior is akin to listening to a sports talk show.

Values

For purposes of thoughtful reflection, it is essential to distinguish the differences between views and values. Values are things that we desire, what we individually tend to prize or regard as worthy. For example, each one of us values different aspects of sport participation. However similar, we each bring our individual interpretations of sport's worth to the field. One person may value winning at any cost, while another values the collaborative interaction of opponents playing in a tightly contested game.

VALUES tend to be emotionally charged wants and desires. Values may or may not be moral/ethical and may or may not be transmitted into action.

Values are personal choices, relative to our own individual thoughts and feelings. It is important to understand that personal values are not always ethical. Values are subjective. They differ from person to person and are more a matter of preference than principle. They may be right for a person, but not necessarily right and just for all people involved in the sports program. If a group of people, a team, an organization, parents, coaches, student-athletes or a league holds similar values in sport participation, it doesn't necessarily mean that these shared values are right and just. Sometimes, the moral consensus favors elitism and "must win" values at the expense of player's enjoyment and satisfaction. Russell Gough, a sports philosopher, once said, "you can play by all the rules, and still be unethical."

Virtues — Core Ethical Values On and Off the Field

Core values, or virtues, are considered universally desirable habits to which we hope all the people involved in the athletic program will aspire. These core values consist of, but are not limited to, the formation of a person's character through the learning of such traits as respect, responsibility, integrity (consistency of action), justice (fair play and respect for others), courage (founded in self-discipline, patience and perseverance), moderation/balance, and care and compassion. As mentioned in chapter 3, the core values of US Lacrosse are connection, leadership, respect, tradition, spirit, trust and youth. The healthy formation of an athlete's character, like the acquisition of a sport skill, requires hard work, consistent and faithful practice, patience, perseverance, constant striving for improvement, and respect for the advice of coaches, knowledgeable parents and peers. Coaches, parents and program directors strongly influence character development through the ideals and actions they present. To instill a sense of right knowledge and action requires thoughtful reflection to produce consistent behavior. The US Lacrosse "Standards of Excellence" are embedded in the virtues approach:

- maintain the traditions and culture of the sport
- assure the continuing education and safety of all participants
- promote sportsmanship and character development
- maintain responsible administration and commercialism for lacrosse

VIRTUES are commonly accepted positive traits that transcend most creeds, cultures and communities. They are habits of the mind, heart and action and are always ethical/moral.

Scenario 1

Two coaches are discussing the merits of the town's youth lacrosse program. They're specifically speaking about a member of the town's under-12 travel team, an 11-year old girl who is not seeing much playing time. At first, this didn't concern her. However, she is now becoming more disengaged from the process and not sure if she wants to stay with the team.

VIEWS APPROACH

When it comes down to the wire, you play your strengths. This is an"elite" traveling team. She made a choice. She could play for the house team and get plenty of playing time. It was her call.

Yes, but she made the travel team. Doesn't that imply that she is good enough to play?

The first coach believes that the travel team ought to play the most talented players. The other coach takes issue and claims that a girl who is good enough to make the team should be allowed to play. These points of view can become heated and may not be resolved in a way that benefits the player and the program, in general.

— — — — — — — — — — — — — — — —

VALUES APPROACH

Our town's lacrosse program is exceptional. We have a strong travel team that is highly competitive. That level of play demands dedication to the team. She should hang in there and wait her chance to play.

We value participation on our town's lacrosse program. Therefore, she should be able to get playing time since she made the team.

The first coach declares that perseverance and dedication are important, regardless of playing time. The second coach claims that involvement – having the opportunity to play – is an important value of every team in the town's lacrosse program. Dedication and participation, respectively, are important to each coach. Their individual preferences ought to be tested for consistency with the lacrosse program's stated mission.

－－－－－－－－－－－－－－－－－－－－－

VIRTUES APPROACH

The travel and house teams were formed to provide all our young people with opportunities to play at the appropriate levels. I think we should put her on a local team until she is ready to participate at the next level.

The town's lacrosse program is founded on participation, regardless of ability level. Everyone deserves to play in a balanced and success-conducive environment.

If a core virtue of the program is to value participation, then there is an organizational responsibility to provide appropriate opportunities for involvement. In the virtues approach, the foundation to the discussion is based on virtuous behavior.

Scenario 2

In a high school game (boys' or girls'), the red team's offense, as predicted, is much stronger than the gold team's defense. The gold coach has informed his/her players to stay right on the stick and body (almost holding) of their opponents whether they have the ball or not. The gold team is subtly talented with this movement and is effectively slowing the red team's offense down. Several coaches scouting in the stands are having an interesting conversation.

VIEWS APPROACH

I can't believe the officials aren't calling the tight contact.

It's all part of the game. You have to somehow compensate with these questionable moves to keep the score close. And it isn't illegal unless you get caught!

One coach claims that the holding is a penalty, not in the letter or spirit of the game, and it should be called. The other coach believes that you have to play to your strengths, and that playing on the edge of the rules is part of the game.

— — — — — — — — — — — — — — — —

VALUES APPROACH

The rules of the game state that their actions are not legal, whether they are called or not.

The gold team values perseverance. They do what they can to equalize the playing field. They don't let down.

One coach suggests that the "gold" team is committed to doing what is necessary to win the game. This is a "value" transmitted by the coach to the players. The other coach sees this behavior as "rule-breaking" and flies in the face of honoring your opponent. Both sides clearly declare their "values" – be they misguided or not.

— — — — — — — — — — — — — — — —

VIRTUES APPROACH

The gold team's behavior really neutralizes the red team's strong efforts that are a result of talent, ability and deliberate practice. The red team's effort should not be muted by a decrease in talent, ability and execution by the gold team.

To make the game better, both teams should play to their strengths. However, the gold team's actions are a way to compensate for their lack of talent, ability, and possibly good coaching and should not be allowed.

Note the differences in these scenarios as compared to views and values. The importance of thoughtful reflection on the influence of virtue as a foundation is the prime theme in the discussion. Therefore, if you declare that you run a character-based program, and your actions are based on views and values without regard to virtue, then your means and your ends are not in synch. When this happens, it is a red flag to make sure that the core virtues of the program are known, valued, and acted upon consistently.

5 *The Right Questions* — How do you individually respond to moral dilemmas as a player, coach, official, parent or administrator? How are your team/program values consistent with "virtuous behavior?"

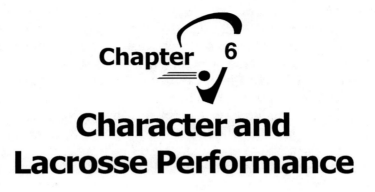

Chapter   6

Character and Lacrosse Performance

The lessons are straightforward: There is no path to excellence
at anything except the deliberate, purposeful formation
of daily habits that make the specific form of excellence
possible. There are no shortcuts, and mere talent is not
enough.

—Edwin J. Delattre – *Sport: A Crucible of Aspiration*

    The relationship between character and performance is seldom addressed. Most coaches are in the business of human performance. At the youth level, we want the players to experience joy and satisfaction through mastering stick skills and fundamental strategies. At the Division I level, we want the players to have individual and team skill sets that, when enacted, produce excellence on the field. However, many coaches still separate the character piece from the actual strategy and task on the field. The two are vitally interconnected. Most people who participate in lacrosse strive to perform well. Regardless of winning and losing, a person's character ought to remain the same. Despite the logical link between character and performance, many coaches continue to consider the myth that paying too much attention to the player's character will soften their focus on performance.

    A lacrosse player who has developed a strong character can call on a foundation of well-formed habits in aspiring to achieve true excellence. The competition on the field, together with a personal goal to optimize performance, challenges the player to continually stretch his or her abilities through deliberate practice – focused and effortful rehearsal. Peter Greer, the former head of school at The Montclair Kimberley Academy in Montclair, N.J., states that "we must will and put into action good habits. We must will improved skills – we cannot wish them to happen." Performance excellence is a direct result of the process, the "means" by which an outcome is achieved. Coaches and athletes who possess good character have a greater opportunity to engage in the deliberate practice necessary to perform well. All stakeholders in the lacrosse program ought to carefully consider this principle, for the well-being of both the players and other participants.

There are many factors that contribute to successful individual and team performance. What separates successful performers from others is the ability to make the most of what they can control in their aspirations for enjoyment, satisfaction and performance. The mental aspect of a lacrosse player's training regime can be an invaluable component for optimizing performance. Mental training skills, such as goal-setting, visualization and attention-control training may provide an effective way to train a player's mind. Specifically, the training enhances performance arousal so the player can be in an optimal state of functioning.

It is important to understand that, although lacrosse performance is measured by the proper execution of fundamental skills, players at any level are not "machines." We are all complex beings with different desires and motives. Performance and satisfaction is influenced by the physical, emotional, mental, moral, social and spiritual (sense of purpose and meaning) factors. All these variables are interconnected. Dee Stephan offers a good example: "Watching my husband play in the Vail Tournament 2003 when his team, CVLC, won the masters division was an incredible experience. He loved every minute of play and we went as an entire family. The four kids loved watching their dad. My oldest daughter even enjoyed watching the women's division games and the girl's high school division which had one of my players on it. I think this sparked her love of the game more than anything else that year. What a beautiful place to play and watch lacrosse!"

Performance Excellence

Deliberate practice that leads to performance excellence requires a good degree of patience and perseverance. More often than not, the initial process of improvement, guided by practice, requires the player to be willing to make choices different from what they "feel like" doing in the moment. "I most fondly remember the routine—the way that lacrosse practice and games became part of my daily life," says Brad Jorgenson, of his experiences as a player at Springfield College.

Athletes who are committed to improving their performance quickly learn that one of the most significant sources of both difficulty and joy comes from the ability to rise to the challenge – they don't back down from heightened levels of lactic acid build-up or momentary lapses in motivation. The ability to stretch beyond one's perceived ability or desire, and to continue is contingent on asking, "What is the *right* action – what needs to be done *at this time* to improve performance – right now?" This allows the second home to have the patience to find the cutting first home; the midfielder to continue playing good defense even though he is exhausted, and the goalie to be ready to save the next shot, regardless of the last two that were scored on him or her. And with this effort also comes the joy and satisfaction of playing lacrosse. When the body and mind adapt to higher demands, the adaptation leads, inexorably, to a heightened sense of engagement, a "dog-with-a-bone" type of satisfaction.

Dave Urick says, "We aspire to performance excellence in terms of the preparation to recruit good student-athletes. Once we get them here, we try to develop them in the off-season with not only their skill development but their physical development. Ultimately, we have to blend that all together to mesh with the other guys and now we have to get the team concepts all in sync with one another."

The Flow State

Mike Csikszentmihalyi's model of flow, the ability to be engaged in and enjoy the process of any endeavor, clearly illustrates the importance of a lacrosse participant's willingness to meet challenges that are marginally equal to or above his or her current skill level (see Figure # 5). If the athlete's skill level is higher than the challenge, boredom sets in. In contrast, when the player's skill level is relatively lower than the challenge, anxiety enters the equation. Only when the challenge meets skill can the individual be fully engaged in and enjoy the endeavor for the sheer sake of participation. When enjoyment is paired with en-hanced sport performance, it is impossible for the relationship between challenge and skill to remain stagnant.

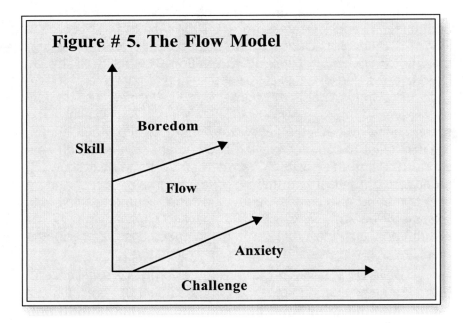

Figure # 5. The Flow Model

It is important for coaches to understand the flow model, in that it reinforces the necessity for athletes to be willing to push beyond what they feel like doing. When experiencing the flow state, the athlete is fully enjoying the process and wants to continue participation.

"Smith" Field of Dreams – The Flow State

The week before our April 4, 1975 home game versus Middlebury, I didn't have one of my best games as we were drubbed 14-8 by Bowdoin. I distinctly remember Charlie Corey, Bowdoin's flashy attackman, lighting me up consistently over the seemingly never-ending match. I was especially disappointed in my play, since Mort LaPointe, the legendary Bowdoin coach, was also on the 1975 North-South All Star Game selection committee. It was now time to redeem myself against a very discliplined Middlebury Panther squad. As we drove our cars over to Smith Field from Boston State (the field was in Brighton, approximately three miles from campus as the crow flies), we found ourselves in gridlock trying to navigate through the traffic just coming into the city for the Boston Red Sox opener (little did they know that they were still 29 years from winning a World Series). As we arrived late for our own home game, Middlebury, in their matching navy helmets, jerseys and shorts were in formation doing their warm-up. I rushed out of Danny Hayes' car (freshman middie) and we went down to the south end of the field to unlock the chain that kept our goals safe from the neighborhood vagrants. My ensuing warm up in the goal was mediocre, and I feared another Bowdoin fiasco. True to these thoughts (I wish I knew as much back then about sport psychology as I do now), Middlebury pumped in two quick goals and at 2-0, I could hear the home crowd of 43 people – I am over exaggerating – muttering the "Oh, no, Yeager sucks today," which I am under exaggerating. However, I stayed the course and took the next shot off my helmet on their man-up, as the small crowd cheered my ability to have my "head" in the right place at the right time. Somehow, I began to feel a bit more in control and several moments later, Middlebury's face-off middie won the draw and charged down towards our goal. He took a hard overhand shot – I anticipated and dropped my stick and caught the ball off the bounce. Immediately motivated, I threw a slightly arced clearing pass to my center middie, who set off on a fast break with two subsequent passes and our first goal. From that moment on, 32 saves later, I was in the zone. The ball seemed to come to me in slow motion. All the sounds around me were muted. The only thing I saw was where the ball was on the field. It was an incredible feeling of "flow" as we won the game, 6-2. Although it was almost 30 years ago that this event happened, and I probably have embellished it slightly (aging, you know), that event stands out for me as a defining moment. Not only in lacrosse for me, but as a motivator in my life that I bring up when needed.

— John Yeager

Unfortunately, the flow state is not the dominant experience in sport. During the more difficult differentiation moments, when the challenge is slightly beyond the player's comfort level, some athletes simply do not have the capability needed to rise to the occasion. Others are able to draw on the habits of good character they have previously formed. This makes it much easier to make the right choices in the moment – not what they feel like doing, but what needs to be done.

Many lacrosse players are unaware that these character traits are summoned to action at the critical moments in a practice or a game. They remark that they just did what they needed to do, a result of ritual and deliberate practice. It is important to note that many athletes and coaches do not think about this process much, since deliberate practice may be second nature. The work ethic has been engraved in such a way that undertaking the task is a measure of their character. "Your best player may not always be your hardest worker and the opposite holds true. However, when it all comes together, they are rewarded for their perseverance through the hard times," says Chris Paradis.

Steve Koudelka remembers this to be true when he experienced his team play Washington and Lee in the 2003 Old Dominion Athletic Conference championship game at Lynchburg. "It poured down rain Friday and into early Saturday. Most of the team had to remove the rain tarps from the field 90 minutes before face-off. There was a huge crowd watching us down at halftime, down going into the fourth. We finally tied the game with seven minutes left and won in overtime 6-5. This was the first lacrosse championship in school history and gained Lynchburg the automatic berth into the NCAA tournament. Watching the team take the tarp off the field before the biggest game of their careers, I sensed they would play great that day. Each player seemed to have this look of being in the zone."

I asked Dave Pietramala, the head men's coach of 2005 NCAA Men's Division I champion Johns Hopkins, how he and the Hopkins team reacted when UVA scored with little time left in the 2005 semifinal game. "I immediately turned and went to the box to get Kyle Harrison. At the same time, Greg Peyser, the Hopkins face-off man, says 'I got this one. I got it. I am going to get this for you.' OK! Nobody panicked – we had been there before. They just believed in each other. All the time, the effort and the energy we put in led to this opportunity. Since I came to Hopkins, we are 21-5 in one-goal games. Our players believe in what we do – the little things we do every day." This is a prime example of deliberate practice reaping great rewards.

Deliberate Practice and the Flow Experience

Being rewarded with a strong performance as a result of consistent deliberate practice is the most satisfying part of the game for my players. They want to compete and compete at a high level. They know that they need to put their best foot forward to be able to accomplish this. The desired result is obviously to come out with at least one more goal than the other guy and, when that happens, you take some measure of satisfaction from it. But you realize that everything you did that day wasn't perfect, and one of the things that we tell our guys here is that lacrosse is a game of mistakes. We can't really worry too much about making mistakes. We make a big distinction between making errors of omission and errors of co-mission, and that is a big part of our approach to the game.

When we do come up short and have a game that doesn't end up with the desired result, the thing that I look at first and foremost is the effort. If we put forth the type of effort that I think we needed to or were capable of and we lost that game, then we just deal with it and realize that we played as hard as we possibly could that day, but we just didn't win. We didn't have enough that particular day. It is just the way it is. If you don't get the effort then maybe there is a chance that you want to factor in other issues and start to look harder into why you didn't have that effort on that particular day. That is the key part for me. I don't get crazy when we lose, unless I feel we just didn't give the effort that we needed. That doesn't happen very often because of the people I have been fortunate enough to work with. I am not sure that that is the type of approach that will win you a national championship, but it is the one that I am comfortable with.

—*Dave Urick, Head Men's Coach, Georgetown University*

These thoughts are echoed by Mike Wilcox, a member of the US Lacrosse Foundation, an organization charged with developing capital and financial support for US Lacrosse. He believes that deliberate practice on the field carries over into one's personal and professional life. As a former college-All American and North-South Game participant, Mike claims the "hours after practice – shooting and shooting and shooting; learning to improve my game – both ways. That ethic creates excellence and spills over to your personal life and your business life. It is the feeling of being two goals down with a minute to play and knowing what you have to do to get back in the game. This can help a person through a traumatic personal situation or a business challenge. You have been there before. Through that work ethic, you find there are no shortcuts. And you find that ones who try to take shortcuts in life and business suffer the same consequences as those who take shortcuts on the field."

Factors of a Skilled Lacrosse Performance

Although some people may be born with exceptional athletic ability, a combination of many factors contributes to developing a skilled experience. Leonard Zaichkowsky, a leading sport psychologist with college and professional teams, and Jerry Larson, former head of school at Cheshire Academy, break a performance down into six primary factors that support the development of a skilled performance (see Figure #6). These include fitness, physical endowments, motor skills, cognitive understanding, sport skill, and psychological factors. Most of these factors, beyond obvious constraints such as height, can be enhanced through both physical and mental practice.

First, successful performers need to be fit. This factor can be further divided into cardiorespiratory endurance, muscular strength and endurance, and flexibility. Second, physical endowments, such as physique, weight, height and vision, have important implications. Third, motor skills, including speed, reaction time, agility and coordination, are critical. Forth, cognitive understanding of time and space—how one reads and reacts to situations—influences performance. Fifth, athletes need to develop their sport-specific skills if they expect to attain their athletic goals. Finally, numerous psychological components contribute to performance. These encompass formation of traits such as commitment, desire to excel, desire to win, self-confidence, emotional stability and self control. Excellence in sport requires the necessary amount of motivation, task-appropriate physical attributes and adequate social support.

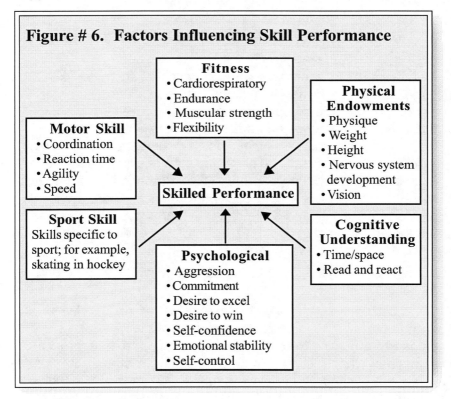

Figure # 6. Factors Influencing Skill Performance

Fitness
- Cardiorespiratory
- Endurance
- Muscular strength
- Flexibility

Physical Endowments
- Physique
- Weight
- Height
- Nervous system development
- Vision

Motor Skill
- Coordination
- Reaction time
- Agility
- Speed

Skilled Performance

Sport Skill
Skills specific to sport; for example, skating in hockey

Psychological
- Aggression
- Commitment
- Desire to excel
- Desire to win
- Self-confidence
- Emotional stability
- Self-control

Cognitive Understanding
- Time/space
- Read and react

Some players are able to compensate when there is a deficit in one or more "factors." Nick Antol, an assistant coach at Portsmouth Abbey in Middleton, R.I., and a former Division I goalie at Notre Dame, had the opportunity to work with a goalie last season who had some physical challenges that prevented him from running well. Nick commented that his goalie compensated for his diminished running ability and foot agility with exceptional lacrosse skills, upper body motor skills, psychological skills and cognitive understanding. "He is a gamer, and stayed focused in the goal every moment," says Nick. "Although the back up goalie had better fundamentals, he was such a hard worker, it made up for any of his athletic shortcomings. He could effectively and efficiently throw right- and left-hand outlet passes and make things happen during the transition. This resulted from countless hours of wall ball."

Performance Arousal

Yuri Hanin, a professor at the Research Institute for Olympic Sports in Jyvaskyla, Finland, has conducted extensive research in the area of performance arousal. The results show that sometimes coaches and athletes are too uptight, too psyched up for a contest – meaning that they are over-aroused. In extreme over-arousal, the physiological signs include increased heart rate, racing thoughts, profuse sweating and tense muscles which may result in relatively poor performance. There are other times when coaches and athletes are under-aroused – meaning they are in a lethargic, "I don't care" state of mind and performance is again adversely affected.

The model in Figure # 7 illustrates how players respond to arousal differently.

Each player has a certain level of "zone" or "bandwidth" in which they have the capacity to perform optimally. Athletes respond to arousal differently. For some, it is best to approach competition when feeling calm and relaxed. For others, they need to be more excited. Some players do best when they are highly charged. For each type of athlete, performance is optimized at low, medium or high levels of arousal, and this continuum of arousal levels will differentially influence performance. For all types of players, at their lower end of the continuum, when under aroused, performance tends to be poorer. As arousal is increased, performance tends to increase. This is where the athlete can enter a flow state, maintaining the right amount of arousal to be at his or her best. That is the state where the player wants to be.

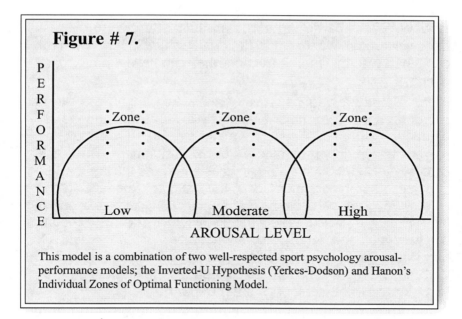

Figure # 7.

PERFORMANCE / AROUSAL LEVEL

Zone — Low
Zone — Moderate
Zone — High

This model is a combination of two well-respected sport psychology arousal-performance models; the Inverted-U Hypothesis (Yerkes-Dodson) and Hanon's Individual Zones of Optimal Functioning Model.

Concentration and Attention Control

Lacrosse players, coaches and officials who are able to perform in a flow state tend to maintain a high level of concentration and attention, i.e., a state characterized by the absence of distraction. *Distraction* is a key word, since the goal of performing well is to minimize anything that takes the athlete's mind away from the task at hand. Generally, when people are doing something well they are experiencing very low levels of distraction. Research claims that when distraction goes up, performance goes down – a correlation that applies to the game of lacrosse. Dave Urick says that the "ball is hot" – this is where the action is – and the ball can move around the field north to south and east to west so quickly that player distraction can be the difference between a goal or a save and subsequent successful clear. It is very subtle.

The relationship works the other way as well. When distraction goes down, performance goes up. The absence of distraction may not be the main reason a lacrosse player, coach or official performs well – other factors influence performance.

However, those participants who are fully attentive to the task at hand will probably perform to their given capabilities. When this is combined with minimal distraction, they can have a pretty good outing.

There are various types of distraction, and these can be categorized into four major areas: physical, mental, social and emotional. The mental category might include, for example, a player's uncertainty regarding his or her assignment. The social category includes such distractions as a player's feeling that he or she doesn't fit in as a member of the team or experiencing a low comfort level when he or she is communicating with the coaching staff. Finally, there are emotional distractions, such as a tough day in school, or a fight with a boyfriend or girlfriend, or with Mom and Dad, prior to a contest. This category also includes situations that may be more serious, requiring professional attention. Keep in mind that these categories often overlap.

Consider a simple illustration by Mark Boyea. The top set of bars, in Figure # 8 that follows, represent the capacity for concentration that accompanies a performance for an elite, average and novice lacrosse player. For example, when the athlete has been injured, awareness and concentration tend to focus on the injury. This distraction eats away at the open space within the bottom set of bars. The more that distractions are allowed to enter the bar, the smaller the open space for concentration gets within the bar. The athlete has less capacity to focus on the task, and the level of performance decreases.

Each participant has a certain amount of available space. The size of the bars will vary from person to person, depending on such factors as motor skills, sports skills, cognitive understanding, fitness level, physical endowments and psychological skills. Elite athletes have larger bars. If they become slightly distracted, they can probably still perform pretty well. Other players, specifically at the youth and high school levels, and with relatively inexperienced coaches, generally have much smaller bars. They can stand only a certain amount of distraction. The higher the level of innate ability and training, the larger the bar is. The implication for coaching is this: You have to know where your players are to know how much and what kinds of distraction they can withstand and still perform well. Inevitably, distraction can temporarily turn an elite player into an average one, and an average player into a novice one. The distracted novice lacrosse player will probably find little joy in his or her performance.

Success for the men's program at Johns Hopkins University is predicated on excellent talent and strategies which are forged by healthy relationships – a sense of trust between coaches and players and players and players – which inevitably reduce distraction and increase attention to what matters most. There isn't a lot of class distinction in the locker room at Hopkins. Players have the word "family" screened on the back of their t-shirts. "We are a family," notes Pietramala. "The head coach is the head of the family and the players need to know that you care about them. The assistant coaches are essential in the trust process and are great buffers in helping keep all communication lines open. We don't select captains until the week before the first fall tournament so the current year's selection includes the freshman."

Pietramala believes in doing the little things such as leaving a note in a player's locker saying, "Hey – did a great job today." It is amazing what little things can do.

He claims that "success" can be measured by the traffic that comes through the coach's office. "We have players in and out of our office all day long. There is a candy jar in the office and players come in and grab a piece and sit down and start chatting. In fact, a group of players would come in every Thursday and would have lunch."

6

✓ *The Right Questions* — As a coach, what are the individual and team distractions that can be minimized to help increase performance?

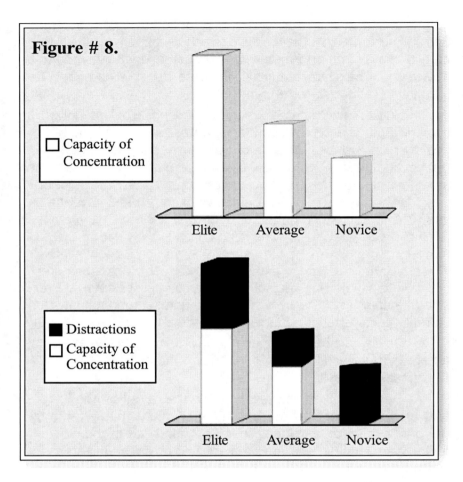

Figure # 8.

☐ Capacity of Concentration

Elite   Average   Novice

■ Distractions
☐ Capacity of Concentration

Elite   Average   Novice

The concepts of attention and distraction relate to character in many ways. Trust is a good example. An individual's ability
to trust the person at the next level above them is critical. This
involves the player-to-coach relationship as well as coach-to-
athletic director relationship, and the athletic director-to-principal/
head of school relationship. When things get tight on the field,
even a small amount of doubt can take some of the space in the
bar away. The more distracted a player or coach may be, the
greater the likelihood of making a bad decision. It is important for
the program administrator and coach to relate to the people who

report to them, and trust them. If not, the coach or administrator has played a part in creating distraction and decreased the opportunity for success.

Trust also applies to action on the field. When a player is not sure about the preparation of a fellow teammate, doubt begins to creep in. This may distract the athlete at a critical time and diminish the likelihood of the team performing at its best.

The same principle applies in the case of caring. Caring is synonymous with "mattering," with the sense that other people are important and that we should be concerned with their well-being. Coaches and other lacrosse stakeholders not only need to trust the people they work with, they also need to care about those people – to be truly concerned with the player's welfare. Coaches can be demanding, but still show that they are concerned about the athlete. A great example is Bill Tierney, head men's coach at Princeton, who is very demanding of his players' reinforcement of fundamentals and the deliberate practice of team strategies. In turn, their execution is typically exceptional on game day. This caring promotes a reciprocal trust that supports each other to collectively get the job done.

Adult mentors can't fake a caring attitude – players can smell phony behavior a mile away. They know if a coach is not authentic and genuine. Program administrators and athletic directors ought to be aware of this when they recruit new staff members. If you want your program to reach its potential, you need to be concerned about bringing on coaches who demonstrate genuine concern for the welfare of the team and overall program.

However, it should be noted that there are lacrosse coaches who are not "good" people. They are the minority, but they do exist. It is important to understand that most coaches are not talented enough to overcome a deficient character. The bottom line is that a coach's character will influence performance. To cite the famous "Dirty Harry" cliché: "Do you feel lucky? Do you think you are really that good that you can get away with and overcome creating your own distractions through deficient character habits? If I am playing for you and I can't trust you, it may be a potential distraction. In a tight game, mistrust creates a moment of doubt – a moment of hesitation in carrying out your directions as a coach." The potential is there! Therefore, coaches can't afford to be sloppy. Do you want to take the risk?

Communicating for Successful Performance in the Developing Lacrosse Player

What increases trust and decreases distraction is the ability for coaches to ensure that the players clearly understand the instructions and feedback provided. Different players at all levels have different ways of accessing information from the coach. Some are visual and learn through observation. Some pick up on the sound of the coach's voice or whistle, while others best pick up kinesthetic cues and learn best through actually doing the drill or activity.

It is especially critical at the youth level to allow aspiring players access to this information. It is important for coaches to provide this information in a language that young people can understand. John Pirani suggests using figurative speech such as "running to space" or "running to bubbles" or making "bridge passes." Young players may better understand what a bridge looks like and then can effectively arc his or her pass. In boys' lacrosse, he will tell a player covered on the weak side of the defense, "to get out of the shadow." This is a visual cue that means the same thing as "triangulating." Visualization works better for an 11-year-old. A player once gave him a quizzical look in trying to understand the "shadow" concept, so Pirani resorted to using planetary terms related to an "eclipse" to bring the technique to life.

Sometimes we may make the assumption that the players understand what we are trying to convey in the huddle. In fact, this can be evident at all levels of the game. So, it is important to see if individuals and the group comprehend the intended message. This can be done in a healthy and non-condescending manner. There may be some indicators that players are not "getting it." It is important to get to the kids level," says Lou Corsetti. "I will sit on the ground with them or take a knee to be at the players' eye level while they are standing, as opposed to being portrayed as this big authority figure. I also give players nicknames that they really take to, such as 'Scooter' for a fast player."

John Sardella is an elementary school principal, former president of the Brine Upstate Lacrosse League and currently very active in the Liverpool (N.Y.) youth league. He believes it is very important when working with young people between grades three and eight to ensure that they have an understanding of the expectation of various drills and strategies. "I always bring them in to discuss what the current practice will entail and then review the previous practice," says John. "It is important to ask questions regarding the drill and strategies, so the young players can echo back what they have learned and then demonstrate the move-ment." This type of critical thinking allows for the coach to see if the players actually understand what they are doing. Response and demonstrations reinforce the skill set.

John Pirani suggests that successful youth coaches are energetic, clear and concise in their communication with players. He says, "Provide them the information and then put them in small groups or short lines to execute skill – a line of three instead of a line of eight players. It is easier to check for understanding in shorter lines. Besides, longer lines are "deadly" to the learning and motivation process. Lou Corsetti and many other coaches employ the "part – whole" concept – a wonderful way of providing young players a structured mind/muscle training strategy to improve catching and throwing skills.

Performance tends to increase when players are briefed at the beginning of practice so they all have a good sense of know-ing: what they are going to do; why they are doing it; and how they are going to do it. Therefore, coaches ought to plan out practices whether they are working with the youngest players or elite athletes. Briefing the players at the beginning of practice and debriefing them after the cool-down stretch is a demonstration of respect for them and their efforts, and can result in great rewards on the field. Pre-planning in this manner really "seals the deal" on an effective practice.

It is essential that youth coaches be able to communicate effectively with their charges. Many of the youth coaches that John Sardella brings in are also schoolteachers, who are professionally trained in knowing how and when to disseminate information and how to see the big picture – from the anticipatory set to the culminating event of a practice. It is very important to mentor new coaches who are non-teachers in how to effectively and efficiently break down a skill for young players.

Lou Corsetti believes that equating some strategies and techniques to other sports can help youth players gain better grasp. Basketball is a great example, as when sprinting down the court with the back to the hoop. Lacrosse is similar, just with a larger playing surface. Learning how to throw can be equated to the actions of a baseball pitcher. "By demonstrating how other sports relate to lacrosse, it provides the young player with a better understanding," says John Sardella

Having fun is part of the mission and Corsetti presents some "goofy" drills such as "lights out," where players pass the ball with their eyes closed. This helps them focus on the fundamentals of keeping the arms away from the body and keeping the feet in the right position. This helps the players get a feel of what it is like to make a ten yard pass. (Of course, they keep their eyes open to catch the ball!) Also, to simulate the dynamic balance aspects of catching and throwing on the run, Lou has introduced a game called "Mr. Miyagi" (from *The Karate Kid*). Players will stand still and catch and throw with one foot. When asked about the value of this drill, he reminds his players that most catches and throws on the run will have a foot off the ground or just landing or taking off.

Casey Jackson, whose lacrosse journey has taken her from New England to Colorado, believes that good youth coaches find ways to play weak and strong players who are on the same team. She says that the number one question she receives from coaches is: "What do I do with my weak player. How do I hide her?" She immediately replies, "You have to get her out from being hidden, because she wants to hide, too." Casey claims that you have to help "Suzie Sizzlebritches" come to an understanding of her own gifts. On the flip side, you may have "Rhonda Rockstar" – who wants to win a national title. You have to know how to tame her and challenge her without letting her take the ball all the time. This is about teaching the stronger player to adjust to her other teammates. "If they go coast to coast or ignore an open player and take a one-on-one, then they sit with me." Good coaches who are competent and passionate are better coaches when they are compassionate to the needs of their players. When this happens, distraction is minimized and trust increased.

It is important for coaches, parents, administrators and officials to understand the developmental process of lacrosse players. There are many different variables associated with each athlete. There are dynamic differences between boys and girls, men and women, be they physical, emotional, mental, moral, social and/or spiritual (sense of purpose and meaning).

One size doesn't fit all, and good coaches and other caring adults need to understand and account for the maturational differences in their players. Len Zaichkowsky and Jerry Larson say that "maturation implies a time component that marks the rate of progress towards the developed state."

During childhood, the aspiring lacrosse player is exposed to the manipulative skills of catching and throwing. This is a time of gross and fine motor development. Also, as the child grows, he or she gets a better sense of dynamic balance – stability. "During the early childhood years, children develop what are called *general fundamental skills* of locomotion, stability and manipulation," say Zaichkowsky and Larson.

During childhood (ages 6-9), there is a significant increase in muscle coordination in both boys and girls that complements their skeletal-muscular growth. At this time, children's motor skill development is in a "transitional" phase. Gordon Webb, my college lacrosse coach and retired professor of human movement at the University of Massachusetts at Boston, states that a child's behavioral characteristics are fairly well formed by the time he/she reaches the age of 6. It is difficult to change the behavior of the child once these characteristics are strongly ingrained. However, behavior can be changed, if two factors are present. One is sufficient time and the other is a strong role model.

As boys' and girls' lacrosse players enter late childhood (ages 10-12), they begin to graduate from functional and transitional skills to the formation of lacrosse-specific skills. Zaichkowsky and Larson caution coaches on being attentive to their youth players' difference in timing of their developmental changes. They say, "It should be pointed out that the age range for each phase of motor development shown should be viewed as general boundaries only. Individual differences in motor development can be greatly related to genetic make-up, rate of maturation and background experiences. For example, it is quite possible for a 10-year-old girl to be functioning at the specialized stage in the sport of gymnastics because of her talent and early experience; however, she may be at an early stage of fundamental motor control in activities such as throwing and catching."

At the conclusion of childhood, whether we think of development as a series of stages or as a process of transitions through maturation, the young person has been attempting to navigate towards independence. He or she probably has achieved adequate separation from his or her parents, and he or she is moving from an egocentric perspective of the world to one that allows him or her to understand the world as separate from him or herself. Robert Kegan describes this ability to perceive a separate world by his "principle of durable categories" in which things, people, and self are appreciated as independent entities.

As 11- and 12-year-olds express a greater sense of independence, parents and coaches ought to be attentive to their shift from childhood. For what might look like an assured, confident player on the field may be a fearful young adolescent. Zaichkowsky and Larson agree that "this period can also be characterized as a time when psychological factors can greatly influence motor development and vice-versa." The specialized stage of motor development continues through adulthood.

As adolescents navigate their journey towards adulthood, they adjust to the social norms of their generation on and off the field. They look to the high school, college and national team players who carry the ball with finesse and élan. They are very attentive to social norms that are observed in their friends' and teammates' behavior.

The adolescent challenge, as Kegan points out, is to achieve the status of being an adult, to navigate one's way from childhood to adulthood. The teenager must move from dependence on parents to dependence on self, and then move from a relationship with self to relationships with others. The adolescent is positioned in the middle stage of the "fusion—differentiation—integration" construct.

The journey from childhood to adulthood does not always happen without incident. As Kegan asserts, we are asking a great deal of a young person who by definition is struggling with observations and emotions about self and others, to see him or herself in a context which makes sense of the world. Some teens may have been appropriately supported and challenged or may have dealt with their adolescent guilt or fears competently enough to be ready to "identify inner motivations, hold onto emotional conflict internally, be psychologically self-reflective, and have a capacity for insight..." Most have not. The young person must move from one identity and understanding of subject (self) and object (other) to developing a more sophisticated cognitive response. This is a psychological as well as intellectual challenge. To be able to identify oneself as object, with perspective, is to begin to achieve the goal of adolescent development. This may be the reason high school students struggle with the college essay assignment to write about themselves objectively.

Albert Bandura, a noted behavioral psychologist, believes that young people who have built up their self-efficacy during childhood, through mastery experiences, have a better chance of a smooth transition through adolescence as they try on adult roles with the support of families and friends who share their values. Bandura acknowledges that adolescence is fraught with social, sexual (puberty) and educational challenges. He also admits that physical changes in the adolescents may cause doubt, uncertainty and/or fear from the loss of control that comes with change. However, if a young person has located "sources" of what Bandura refers to as "personal enablement," he or she will be well positioned to enjoy the journey.

Adolescence may not always be the time to establish or reinvent one's identity, but it certainly does provide the opportunity to solidify one's basic beliefs in and sense of self. The challenge is to find those "sources of enablement," to help the individual through the process of becoming. Relationships with significant "others" may provide such support, but there is one aspect of the adolescent condition that may make such relationships difficult, especially for boys.

John Buxton supports Kegan's assumptions and believes that not all teens implode under the stress of their sexual, social and familial odysseys. However, even for the most "competent," the most "self-efficacious," and the most "engaged," sorting out identity and relationship questions alone feels difficult. Therefore, if adolescents hope to emerge from this transitional process un-scathed, or at least reasonably prepared to address the chal-lenges of adulthood, they need support. Some are fortunate to have enlightened parental support, but even they need the assistance of caring adult "others" who will model positive behavior and act as mentors for them. However, if the objective is not merely to survive the journey but to prevail—to enter adulthood as a responsible, balanced person with the capacity to care for oneself and others, then the question of an appropriate training model must be considered.

Research on the "flow state" concludes that there are many teens that experience adolescence successfully. They tend to be those who learn to commit large amounts of energy to difficult tasks and who persevere because they enjoy the chal-lenges they confront. Mike Csikszentmihalyi and his colleagues attempted to discover what motivated successful adolescents to refine, rather than abandon, their talents during these transitional years. The answer was complex, but there were correlations between an adolescent's ability to balance challenge and skill (to find a "flow" experience) and the benefit an adolescent received from having inherited certain family traits and skills. Their research also reinforced the importance of viewing adolescence from a dialectical perspective in which the challenges of integration and differentiation had to be undertaken. As the adolescent considers himself or herself as a changing person —socially and sexually — he or she must also find stability in new relationships and under-standings. Stability and change are not mutually exclusive; rather, they are interdependent.

Elite Lacrosse Performance

What separates successful performers from others is the ability to make the most of what they *can* control in their aspira-tions for optimal performance. This doesn't mean that anyone can become an elite athlete. But it does mean that athletes can strive to perform to the best of their ability levels – aspiring to excellence as individuals and as members of a team. Malcolm Gladwell's August 1999 article in *The New Yorker*, "The Physical Genius," supports these assumptions (see quote below). The "physical genius" wills performance, rather than wishes it. Deliber-ate practice requires concentration and doing what needs to be done. This provides the athlete with the knowledge of what to do at the right moment on the playing field.

What sets physical geniuses apart from other people, then, is not merely being able to do something but knowing what to do – their capacity to pick up on subtle patterns that others generally miss. This is what we mean when we say that great athletes have a "feel" for the game, or that they "see" the court or the field or the ice in a special way. If you think of physical genius as a pyramid, with, at the bottom, the raw components of coordination, and, above that, the practice that perfects those particular movements, then this faculty of imagination is the top layer. This is what separates physical genius from those who are merely very good.

Adam Naylor, a sport psychologist at Boston University, claims the ultimate goal for many who participate in organized athletics, from adolescence to adulthood, is to compete at the highest levels of performance. Excellence in sport requires the necessary amount of motivation, task-appropriate physical attributes, and adequate social support. Naylor cites the work of Czikszentmihalyi and Howard Gardner which suggests that striving for excellence extends beyond physical practice and a youthful beginning. The environment in which one practices and competes must support the sporting mission and nurture it. Naylor says, "beyond understanding an individual's athletic development, one must be sure to consider the process of general human development." Lacrosse players are not only competitors in the athletic arena, but also human beings.

Csikzentmihalyi and Gardner are "quick to point out that excellence is never the property of an individual alone," says Naylor. The environment in which one lives and competes provides guidance to the athlete. Competence at any sport skill develops through the teaching of skills by others. If skills are taught at the appropriate times, by good teachers, athletes will move toward mastery of a sport with few developmental roadblocks (i.e. dropping out of sport, failure to achieve goals). In examining high achievers, they have personally documented the support and guidance of parents, siblings, teachers and others in their social environment.

Parents and coaches are essential in the sporting environment. Their two principle roles in the athlete's development are: instruction and social support. Both coaches and parents provide verbal feedback and model behaviors critical to the athlete's success.

To further understand the environment that surrounds excellent individuals, Csikzentmihalyi believes that it is critical to look at three developmental elements: the individual; the domain; and the field. The individual has certain inherent talents, specific goals, and the intangible "rage to learn." In sport this is the athlete. The field is the environment in which one grows and matures—more specifically, the people and institutions that render judgments on the quality and value of one's work. Examples of elements of the field for the athlete are coaches, parents, teammates, and officials. Lastly, the domain involves the challenges of the endeavor one embraces and its unique opportunities and constraints. The domain is the sport in which one trains and competes. Without understanding these three elements, one cannot sufficiently understand the development of excellence.

The College Recruitment of Great Players with Great Character

Dave Pietramala, arguably one of the best defensemen ever to step on a college field, believes, "The first impression is made when you see a player on the field. You are evaluating his ability. That is what is going to make the player stand out."

Character and the Right Fit

When we eventually meet with a recruit, we tend to talk less about lacrosse and more about their friends, family, other sports and things he likes. The important question needs to be answered: Is this the kind of man we want to bring to Johns Hopkins University – one who will understand his responsibilities in the classroom and on the field? Come and visit individually and bring your family – we sit with them face to face. Educate them on Hopkins. We want a student-athlete who looks you in the eye, is inquisitive, and is a good listener. Our players meet the recruits and have said about some recruits, "I am not sure he fits here at Hopkins." So we look to find the right guys who are great people and who will be great teammates. This is huge for Hopkins. We have shied away from some very talented players because they didn't bring the "character" piece to the table.

My best advice for prospective student-athletes and their parents is for them to be honest. Recruiting is not a game. If there is a school you like, continue to talk. A good coach would do same thing. If you are not interested, don't mislead. This is a very careful line that parent's have to walk.

—Dave Pietramala, Head Men's Lacrosse Coach, Johns Hopkins University

---

However, Pietramala offers this measurement as only the tip of the iceberg. Although the first look at talent is needed, it is not the most important piece of the puzzle. "A lot of talented players catch our eye, but then we look to find out what kind of person he is. It is kind of a cliché, but we look to see what kind of character and family he has, and how he interacts with other players. If he is an offensive player, does he celebrate with his teammates – or point to himself when something good happens? His success can not happen fully on his own. Does he run off the field, or when put down immediately gets back up? He doesn't finger point. These are what we call the "little things," but they carry a lot of weight in our recruiting process." Bob Shriver, head boys' coach at Boys' Latin in Baltimore and the U.S. Under-19 coach in 2003, mentors top high school players and their parents about the need to "be the best you can be" in all areas of the game – on and off the field. He is blessed in many ways to have great players at Boys' Latin. However, this sets up a very competitive situation, as making the varsity squad directly impacts their college recruitment potential.

Drinking, Drugging – Character and Lacrosse

Peter Lasagna is not bashful about his stance on the influence of heavy drinking on lacrosse performance. When he addressed the potential of drinking less, a rising Bates junior uttered, "I think everyone would do it if they knew we would win more." Perhaps not coincidentally, the Bates' captains made restricted alcohol use a much bigger issue than it had ever been before and the team had the most successful season in Bates lacrosse history. Lasagna claims, "I am learning that we are never done with this issue. Many of these players will forget that being better to their bodies translates directly into better practices and games. We will make a large issue of it again this year and every year."

Lasagna, who has been quoted in *Inside Lacrosse* magazine on this topic, supports the groundbreaking research that John Underwood has brought regarding alcohol and marijuana use among college men's lacrosse players. Underwood claims that "team 24- and even 48- hour drinking rules" are only a myth, because many players do not totally physiologically recover by game time. In fact it may take as long as two weeks for a total recovery in some student-athletes.

No Moment Is Recoverable – A Lost Opportunity

At the risk of getting personal, I am compelled to share one of my greatest regrets regarding my lacrosse career. In 1981, I was fortunate to be selected as one of the top eight men's goalies in the country to attend the 1982 U.S. men's team tryouts during two successive weekends at Penn State. I was playing the best lacrosse of my life with the Brine team (out of Boston). We had double and triple sessions, which dealt with one vs. ones, two vs. twos, three vs. threes, half field and full field scrimmaging. By the middle of day two during the first weekend, I was playing well and thought that I was in the middle of the pack. My hope was to be one of the top four goalies – two chosen for the team that would play in the ILF World Championship and two alternates to play on the U.S. "B" Team. However, by that evening, I was really tired, not focusing and was literally "destroyed" in a scrimmage in front of 20 observant coaches. The next day was no better. What I finally realized in the long ride home to Massachusetts at the end of the weekend, was that I had become so dehydrated on the field, that my play suffered. The weekend prior to the tryouts, I spent a long night drinking with other lacrosse players celebrating my upcoming trip to Penn State. I didn't recover from that weekend until after the first weekend of tryouts. Now, recovery time differs with different people's physiology. However, I had one shot at making the team and I blew it! I will always wonder what might have happened if I was better prepared for the tryouts. Instead I was just a "World Team Wannabe!"

—*John Yeager*

Problem drinking has been a cultural issue whose time has come to be addressed. The cliché of "party hard and play hard" is becoming outdated as the level of parity and play in Division I lacrosse increases. "How can you expect to recover today and then perform to your capabilities," says Dave Pietramala. "Our players need to be careful and need to take care of each other."

According to experts at the Boston-based FCD (Freedom from Chemical Dependency) Educational services, a leading provider of substance abuse prevention programs to schools worldwide, "compounding the damage caused by mistaken normative beliefs is something known as anticipatory socialization. It's really a form of daydreaming in which young people imagine (anticipate) acting out normative roles and behaviors that lie ahead. For example, most kids fantasize about what it will be like when they get their driver's license. Older teens may visualize going to college, having their own apartment, or being in a committed relationship. These future-oriented psychological videos are based in large part on normative beliefs (i.e., "all teens get a driver's license"; "all of my friends are going to college"), and play an important role in maturation so long as the anticipated behavior is healthy and pro-social. Anticipatory socialization can be harmful when the projected behavior is risky, unhealthy, or based on mistaken beliefs. For example, if 10-year-olds think that 'all high school students drink,' they will imagine themselves drinking well before they become teenagers."

SECTION 4

The Responsible Administration and Commercialism of Lacrosse

Chapter 7

Walking the Talk —
Program and Team Management

Each one of our institutions is distinctly different and has different ways of conducting business. If we clearly understand what those things are, and we are able to work within that framework, and then surround ourselves with people who want to go places and get things done, then I think we are able to have a really good, successful solid program. This may not necessarily translate into wins all the time, but it provides the ability to achieve, given the parameters in which you operate.

— Sid Jamieson, Former Head Men's Coach, Bucknell

By recognizing the role and power to influence others, those responsible for the administration of lacrosse teams, leagues and clinics at all levels of the game and those who oversee the development have a privilege and an opportunity to provide exemplary leadership. Responsible program administration expands awareness for the sport and demonstrates a commitment to safety.

For lacrosse programs to be authentically successful, it is essential that the administrators of the respective programs ensure that the membership—players, coaches, and parents—act on the established core values in the program's mission statement. When administrators "walk the talk," their actions speak volumes to the players, coaches and parents about the importance of "doing lacrosse right." The mission statement binds those involved on the team and program together in a common purpose. This can provide strong and compelling motivation to act according to the mission's tenets.

Figure # 9. Suggested Goals of Good Lacrosse Administrators

— Establish and maintain communication network with all stake-holders, including coaches, parents, officials, governing body and industry.

— Provide affordable programs to ensure access to the game.

— Provide honest descriptions of programs or services and deliver what is promised.

— Support the recruitment and retention of coaches and officials so as to fill the ever-growing need.

— Do not compromise quality and positive culture for personal gain.

— Provide a visible administrative presence at lacrosse events.

Tom Zacoi, a member of the US Lacrosse Youth Council who runs programs in the Pittsburgh area, claims if there are "no standards there can be no expectations." He says, "Communication is job #1 outside of protecting the physical and emotional well-being of the players." He supports a healthy credo of coaches and administrators "aspiring to train women in the modern game, to treat then with dignity and respect in an environment in which you can make mistakes, and make good decisions under pressure about lacrosse and off-field experiences."

Intrepid Lacrosse Mission Statement

The mission of Intrepid is to promote the growth of girls' lacrosse in the tri-state area; to field competitive teams by developing advanced playing skills, game knowledge, confidence, responsible decision-making, teamwork and good sportsmanship.

The mission will be accomplished by retaining inspirational and dedicated coaches who will professionally and consistently teach the modern game; treat every girl with dignity and respect; recruit the best high school players, stress physical fitness and strive to make Intrepid a fun-filled and positive experience for all members.

Consonant and Competing Motivations

The formal structure of a lacrosse team or program is comprised of all the people who have a "stake" in the success of the program. It is important to decrease any competing motivations of stakeholders, in order to ensure a coherent program.

While few would disagree that all these people (players, coaches, parents, officials, spectators and administrators) play a role in the sports experience, few understand the importance of requiring these groups to engage in the same process of declaring their values that coaches and players do. Miscommunication, criticism and problems result from lack of agreement about what's important and why it's important. Finding common ground begins with the process of identifying the formal structure and working from there to find those values and goals that are compatible with those best represented by the formal structure.

John Buxton reminds us of the history of sports in the United States and claims that many American coaches have always struggled with their concept of sport because it was borrowed and reconstituted with a different cultural perspective. We wanted new challenges, new approaches, and new ways to compete. So, only those who understand how to balance the ideal of the amateur ethic (the mythical way sport used to be) with the need for gratification through victory (the attitude that brought glory as well as disgrace to professional sports through the last century) have been successful as coaches and as mentors. The challenge is to create environments in which both mastery of the appropriate habits and performance are valued and pursued in balance. The relationship between these objectives should not be stated as an either/or proposition. Teams and programs that take care of the issues of character and habit, environments that foster the ethics and morals of the amateur spirit – to play the game with dignity, integrity and respect – are among the most successful on the lacrosse field.

An analysis of responses from coaches and program administrators of a variety of sports that my colleagues and I discovered in writing *Character and Coaching – Building Virtue in Athletic Programs* were profound:

> 1. Coaches are rarely proactive about inviting others who are a part of the formal structure to participate in the sport process through goal setting, helpful communication, or role definition.
>
> 2. Coaches and athletic administrators rarely think that mission statements for teams or programs are needed if the larger organization (league, school, etc.) has one.
>
> 3. Many programs have problems and issues with "winning and performance" because of expectations, and these issues lead to negative reinforcement by parents, coaches, and schools.
>
> 4. Many programs are plagued by the adolescent focus on "self," which makes "Respect for Opponents" and "Commitment to Team" more challenging goals.
>
> 5. Fewer coaches than we would have anticipated are as aware of their opportunities to mentor as they are of their responsibilities to teach the game.
>
> *Reprinted with permission.*

The value of the "Formal Structure" exercise is for those responsible for the success of the lacrosse program (everyone is a stakeholder) to evaluate how consistent player, coach, parent, officials view the program. In other words, what matters most to them. Are there competing motivations that prevent the goals/ mission of the program to succeed? We are all human and have different desires and appetites. We all see lacrosse as offering value to us and others in different ways. When clearly understanding the responsibilities of the stakeholders, is that consonant with the program? The last question is rhetorical. Everyone is responsible, with competent adults taking the lead to model others.

In his manual, *How to Start a Successful Lacrosse Program*, John Sardella states that it is important to keep your organizations at a manageable size! Don't spread your parameters too far; be strong, fair and consistent; control parents. Make sure they know the rules; and, always follow up with all people involved.

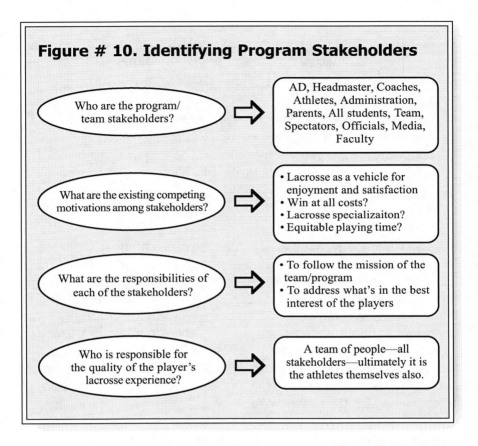

Figure # 10. Identifying Program Stakeholders

| Who are the program/team stakeholders? | ⇒ | AD, Headmaster, Coaches, Athletes, Administration, Parents, All students, Team, Spectators, Officials, Media, Faculty |

| What are the existing competing motivations among stakeholders? | ⇒ | • Lacrosse as a vehicle for enjoyment and satisfaction
• Win at all costs?
• Lacrosse specializaiton?
• Equitable playing time? |

| What are the responsibilities of each of the stakeholders? | ⇒ | • To follow the mission of the team/program
• To address what's in the best interest of the players |

| Who is responsible for the quality of the player's lacrosse experience? | ⇒ | A team of people—all stakeholders—ultimately it is the athletes themselves also. |

Sardella recommends that administrators can ensure a healthy program by "surrounding themselves with good people; getting people who know the game. Lacrosse is not a sport that should be taught by a person with limited knowledge; getting people who can teach the game in a positive manner; encouraging good sportsmanship; and, getting certified officials. Whether they come from scholastic, college or your own league, make sure that they have gone through some kind of certification process to be able to properly officiate a game."

B.U.L.L. Mission Statement

The Brine Upstate Lacrosse League exists to teach Youth in the Central New York community the proper way to play the game of lacrosse while fostering amateur athletic competition from regional to national and international competition. By doing so the league emphasizes sportsmanship and cooperation among all Coaches, Coordinators, Officials, Parents, Players and Volunteers.

Camps and Clubs

I started working at summer lacrosse camps back in the mid-80's and during the beginning of the 90's I found myself owning or co-owning a host of camps in the New England Area. The number of camps has multiplied exponentially. Every spring in their "summer camp" issue, *Lacrosse* magazine encourages camp owners to submit a mission statement and strengths of the camp. Although the statement is brief, it is still a declaration of what the camp promises to provide. This is the credo, a contract that provides a snapshot to players interested in attending and to their parents, most of whom foot the bill.

In many ways, these quick mission statements are 3-second commercials. It is important that the audio meets the video in reality. A variety of statements for the 2005 issue are provided on the next page.

As camp and club programs increase in number, it is important for players and their parents to be good consumers and to ask the important questions of club administrators. What should they look for in a program? Questions should include: What is the mission of the camp or club? What are the expectations? What is the staff/player ratio? What does the camp and club promise to deliver? — An example of the Pittsburgh based "Intrepid" club mission is on the next page.

- The camp to attend to become a better player
- "Elevate your game"
- In-depth shooting for instruction for 2 days
- To provide in-depth goalie instruction
- Learn from experienced coaches
- Fun while working
- Master the space between the pipes!
- We are the Have Fun and Learn How to be Family camp
- Free loaner equipment and All American instruction
- NLL/college coaches teach players the modern game
- One of the best teaching camps you can attend
- A great way for high school students to keep playing
- We want your child to be better, not just entertained
- A fun, instructional camp in an unbeatable setting
- Provide the best instructional camp
- A 6 night 7 day camp that will prepare you for your season
- Fun instruction from college coaches and US players
- Lacrosse meets the Aloha Spirit!
- Teaches fun, innovative lax skills and techniques
- Attacking and Defensive Concepts/Play in the 8M
- SPORTSMANSHIP – TEAMWORK – EDUCATION – PRIDE - SUCCESS
- Scholarships – recruiting
- Camp is focused on individual skills, position work

7 **The Right Questions** — After reviewing the goals in Figure # 9, comment on whether each of the six objectives are being fulfilled within your program—youth, high school, club, collegiate, post-collegiate. If not, why isn't the goal being addressed and how can the goal be realized?

The Survey Says:

Youth level programs in my chapter/region are well-organized with consistent adult support.

		Number of Responses	Response Ratio
Strongly Agree	▅▅▅▅	*463*	*30%*
Agree	▅▅▅▅▅▅	*818*	*53%*
Disagree	▅▅	*217*	*14 %*
Strongly Disagree	▪	*43*	*3%*
	Total	*1541*	*100%*

Shane Murphy, the author of *The Cheers and the Tears – A Healthy Alternative to the Dark Side of Youth Sports Today*, and the former head of the sport psychology program for the United States Olympic Committee, says that administrators who run good youth sport programs should make sure that seven areas of mentorship are covered: start with good coaches; modify the game when appropriate; provide the opportunity to play; introduce competitions gradually; emphasize social interaction; provide variety and interest; and, provide close and exciting contests.

Murphy also addresses the question "What do kids want?" in a youth sports program: "One of the first things I noticed about working with young athletes is that there are tremendous differences among them in the ways they approach sports. Some children are very competitive, others not at all so. Some take the rules seriously while others ignore them. For some children, perfecting a new skill is a serious matter, but others never seem to learn the basics. Underlying these great differences is a variety of motives for participating in youth sports. Sport psychologists have identified several basic themes that occur over and over again when young athletes are asked why they play the game." Murphy cites these themes as "fun, activity and involvement, improvement and skill building, the physical thrill, friendships, social recognition, competition, and attention."

7

The Right Questions — Does the mission of your youth sports program include statements that address having fun, activity and involvement, improvement and skill development, the physical thrill, friendship, social recognition, competition, and receiving attention? If so, how does the administration of the program help make these "statements" come alive in reality? If not, why not?

Chapter 8

The Marketing of Lacrosse

Those responsible for the marketing and distribution of lacrosse products have a privilege and an opportunity to provide exemplary leadership. Responsible commercial marketing of products expands awareness for the sport, demonstrates a commitment to safety, and enables accessibility to the sport.

"The commercialization has become much more part of the sport – now that many more people are playing it," says Marc Van Arsdale, assistant men's coach at the University of Virginia. Youth and high school lacrosse has exploded. And the other thing we see is the "soccerization" of the sport. More and more kids are giving up other sports to play lacrosse all the time – playing fall ball and indoor lacrosse in the winter, instead of football or soccer or basketball. We, as college coaches, continue to try and tell high school players that is not the way to go. We run three sessions of a youth camp at a place called Graves Mountain Lodge, just north of Charlottesville. Each year we talk to the kids about being involved in as many sports as you can, for as long as you can.

This period of growth has led to much more investment in the manufacturing and marketing of lacrosse equipment.

"I think the technological developments in the game have changed the game to a certain degree," says Van Arsdale. "Although I don't go back to the wooden stick, Jerry Schmidt gave me my first lacrosse stick when I moved to Geneva, NY, and my father worked at Hobart. It was one of the first plastic STX models, which is now looked at as an ancient caveman version.

The lacrosse industry walks a fine line in supporting the growth of the game while adhering to the time-tested traditions and culture of lacrosse. Of course, we are aware that some organizations will go to the edge, and at times over the top, to market product, but it is also important to know that equipment safety monitoring continues to improve. US Lacrosse's Sports Science and Safety Committee is getting more involved with equipment safety, but there is still room for improvement in dialogue among the equipment industry and those creating the rules of the game. Chat rooms still echo concerns about the sensationalism and "R" rated versions of marketing is by-product of a larger culture. The membership of US Lacrosse has an opportunity to help guide that culture with their passionate voices about the "how over the top" some products ought to be marketed.

Ricky Fried says he is "glad that some of the lacrosse magazines are kind of backing off because some of the equip-ment ads are just ridiculous in these lacrosse magazines. He, as many others, is concerned with the industry's "use of sexual undertones" with the equipment and obliterate your opponent with the new titanium. The kids will ask me what kind of stick should I use and I tell them, "A lacrosse stick. You aren't good enough to worry about what they're made of yet."

Nevertheless, the modern games are enhanced by the manufacturing of newer, safe and performance-conducive equip-ment. Of course, there are many of us who lament how a pur-poseful and intentional focus on "stick care" had a great influence on how we performed on the field. There is still some truth to that today, but the technology has made the stick easier to care for. And streamlined and safe equipment makes it easier for younger lacrosse aspirants to get hooked.

"I feel the old guard has done a great job of spreading the values and character of lacrosse to the new converts," says Gene Zanella. "The character of lacrosse has maintained itself on the field. The area where the game's character suffers is in the "for profit" areas. Retail stores, camp directors, and the many people who are making a buck off the game of lacrosse have affected its culture in a negative way. These 'for-profit' people convince many youth athletes that the stick or the success they have at an early age will easily lead to a scholarship. Many athletes enter high school believing the greatness they achieved on elite teams is a sure-fire basis for success in high school. These athletes do not understand why a high school coach would make them work on fundamentals when they are already a superstar. Many of these youth greats quickly become frustrated with the new challenges of the high school game."

Marketing the Traditions and Culture of the Sport

It is important for the industry to market products and services that bridge historical cultural with modern culture. The use of marketing techniques that value and reinforce a positive culture for the sport is essential.

Jenny Riitano, at deBeer Lacrosse, claims "The women side has an incredibly deep and rich tradition." Today's rules changes are designed to maximize what athletes are capable of doing. "As girls are starting younger and younger, we design equipment to maximize their ability to perform well. We are changing the game, but trying to make it a little bit easier to keep the enduring culture. As the game evolves, we want to keep the "spirit" of the game alive while making newer products that make it easier for players to play." Although deBeer may have the smallest marketing budget of the major lacrosse manufacturers, they are commitment to promote product from a grassroots position, without a lot of flash and glitch.

Assuring the Continuing Education and Safety of all Participants in the Sport

To assure safety, it is essential for the industry to create products and services that maintain the safety of the players. To go along with the concept of the Red Queen Effect (mentioned in chapter 2) the industry plays an instrumental role in providing safe yet performance-conducive equipment. "Athletes constantly demand 'stronger, faster, lighter' and manufacturers work tirelessly to merge these elements into form, function, and protection," says Adam Werder of Warrior Lacrosse. "By adhering to stringent safety standards, rigorously wear-testing equipment at the level it's designed for and investing heavily in quality control, the safety of equipment is tried and true before reaching the market. Lacrosse is a high-impact sport and manufacturers have a crucial responsibility to earn participants' trust by consistently designing products that maximize safety and performance."

Research and Development ought to be in a collaborative effort with the marketing department. Jenny Riitano says that is essential for the industry to have a very strong relationship with the rules committees. "It is important to meet the specs of product while enhancing certain performance features," she says. The focus is being in alignment with the "letter of the law" in rule making.

In the current environment of change, it is imperative that manufacturers assume the responsibility to communicate regularly with rule makers and coaches. It has become a fundamental role for manufacturers to keep pace with changing rules/expectations and communicate pertinent information to dealers and consumers. There are several bodies responsible for testing of equipment in the men's and women's game, each of which maintains very open and close communication with US Lacrosse. For example men's helmets are approved by NOSCE and women's eye protection by the American Safety Testing methods standards. Also there is an organization, PECC, that helps support the consumer by pulling a product off the shelf to inspect.

Educating the Public on Lacrosse

The industry, in general, works hard to contribute to educating the lacrosse community. Several companies offer programs and services at a grassroots level to educate youth and adults on the game. This, in effect, is a "giving back" to the game that has given to them. In addition, it is important for many of these companies to make sure that their marketing techniques value the culture of the sport.

The Marketing of Lacrosse "Icons"

It is important to honor the traditions of the game as opposed to redefining them. Although change is inevitable and the culture is mandated to change, some traditions ought to be unwavering.

"I feel now that young kids are more fascinated with the personalities in the game than they are with the game's roots," says Dom Starsia. There are a group of great players who have graduated from college and that are now able to make a living in the game. We sort of have our "first rock stars" in lacrosse, and to me, in a lot of ways the game is being marketed that way right now. The manufacturers have a lot to do with that as long as it captures a young kid's imagination.

Endgame — Next Steps

When I step onto the field, whether to play or coach, I have a feeling of calmness and confidence. I am not intimidated or nervous about my opponents or the outcome of the game. I continue to play now in order to meet new people and maintain a satisfactory level of fitness. My life would certainly be different if I did not have the same cultural experiences that lacrosse has offered to me.

—Al Rotatori, Head Boy's Coach at Newton South
  High School, MA

Quality of Experience

Alice Von Hildebrand cites from one of Gabriel Marcel's plays: "Your death is my death." It is true when we lose an important game and realize the finality of a season and the knowledge that our team membership will change, something dies within us. And this can be both painful and fearful. However, as the sorrow abates, we may recognize that the inverse must also be true, that "your life is my life." The things we have taught each other and the memories we created will always keep us connected to each other.

As part of a team, we became landscapers of our terrain. We are influenced by the void many of us feel at this time, in our search to feel and be complete. We continue to search for this completeness in future games and other endeavors, however, our "gift" to each other has helped make our lives a bit more complete. "Stepping over the line" to be fully present in games as players, coaches and parents has helped us experience the emotions of being fully human.

Kevin Hicks, Dean of Berkeley College at Yale and former Brown assistant women's coach, reminds us of an important literary quote he cited at a memorial service for a former Brown player. "Hemingway said it best in *A Farewell to Arms*: 'The world breaks everyone, then some become strong at the broken places.'" We all unite and help each other to become stronger at this one broken place – and this can happen through our shared identities.

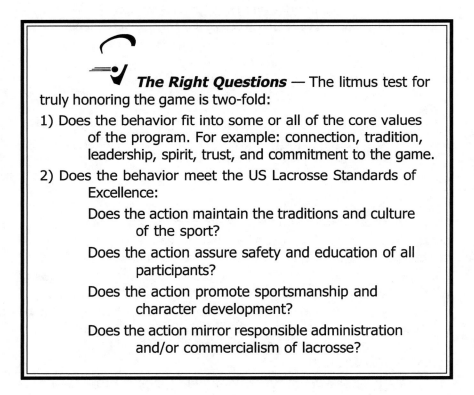

The Right Questions — The litmus test for truly honoring the game is two-fold:

1) Does the behavior fit into some or all of the core values of the program. For example: connection, tradition, leadership, spirit, trust, and commitment to the game.

2) Does the behavior meet the US Lacrosse Standards of Excellence:

Does the action maintain the traditions and culture of the sport?

Does the action assure safety and education of all participants?

Does the action promote sportsmanship and character development?

Does the action mirror responsible administration and/or commercialism of lacrosse?

Robert Kegan, in *The Evolving Self,* describes how important outside influences are in the developmental process. His words provide a fitting conclusion to this book.

One of the important aspects of participating in lacrosse is not only to enjoy life, but also to become a part of it. The pinnacle of participation is just another facet of life in that we merge with life, becoming another part of it and enhancing it.

> *Who comes into a person's life may be the single greatest factor of influence to what that life becomes. Who comes into a person's life is in part a matter of luck, in part a matter of one's power to recruit others, but in large part a matter of other people's ability to be recruited. People have as varying capacities to be recruited as they do to recruit others.*
>
> *And yet however much we learn about the effort to be of help, we can never protect ourselves from the risks of caring, which separate real help from advice, reassurance, or consolation. In running these risks we preserve the connections between us. We enhance the life we share, or perhaps better put, we enhance the life that shares us.*
>
> — *Robert Kegan*

Emily (Buxton) McCann played for Heather Crutchfield at St. Paul's School, NH, and for Carol Kleinfelder at Harvard. She says, "My coaches took the time to develop the "whole woman" – to help position lacrosse as a metaphor for our "work" as members of a community (family, professional). To succeed at the game of lacrosse, you need to trust teammates as much as you trust yourselves to develop a competitive advantage over your competition (because ultimately the ball moves down the field more quickly in the air than in one person's stick). My coaches inspired both an individual and group work ethic that translated powerfully into our non-athletic pursuits."

Dave Pietramala asks his young players at Hopkins to "research the greatest player to ever wear their number."

Lacrosse can and should be a vehicle to authentic happiness. Authentic happiness is the sum of positive emotions, positive traits, and positive institutions. The positive emotions shared in the game are joy, interest, contentment and love. The positive traits are respect, leadership, etc., and the positive institutions mold the tradition, culture, standards of excellence observed in the way we do business on and off the field. This is the prescription for the "full lacrosse life."

> *You come to realize that you cannot survive and win any game without successful connections among teammates. Like the human body, everything needs to connect to succeed. Rivalries never felt bitter in lacrosse because there existed so much respect for the sport and those who love the sport—a shared affection for the simplicity, fluidity and endurance. A great game is like a symphony, keeping pace with the rhythm and flow of the competition.*
>
> —Emily McCann, Former Player at St. Paul's School, NH, and Harvard University

It is the pleasure of playing, coaching and watching the game, and it is the feeling of "flow" through our engagement with others on and off the field. We savor the moments in the game that provide us meaning. And when we ensure that we are involved in the game for the right reasons, then we will find just what we are looking for.

Cradle as you go!

Index

Alessi, Walter 99
Almgren, Jordy 51, 55
Antol, Dave 133, 151
Antol, Nick 151, 152

Battle, Jessica 92
Bigelow, Bob 95
Bohlin, Karen 134, 136
Boyea, Mark 95
Briggs, Larry 82
Bristol, Steve 52, 74, 76, 79, 82, 84
Bugbee, Keith 11, 74, 78
Burbank, Abby 19
Buxton, John 78, 164, 175

Campbell, Dave 50, 94
Cannella, Greg 9, 10, 66
Caravana, Mike 100
Connolly, Steve 67
Corlett, John 38, 39
Corrigan, Kristen 53, 89
Corsetti, Lou 78, 158
Csikszentmihalyi, Mihaly ... 41, 145, 164

Deford, Frank 124, 132
Dillon, Pat 25, 50
Dresher, Kate 19, 26, 52, 106
Drobitch, Justin 91
Dryden, Ken 131

Ebner, Noel 50

Fitz, Jim 15
Foote, Missy 25, 26, 73, 74,
84, 95, 12
Fried, Ricky 14, 54, 98, 184

Gait, Gary 29, 112
Ganzenmuller, Susie ... 25, 26, 30, 54,
79, 104,109, 111, 112, 122, 124
Garber, Dick 66, 67
Gill, Conor 105
Gough, Russell 137

Graham, Will................................. 55
Greer, Peter 144
Grube, Jim 2

Hicks, Kevin 33, 118, 190
Hill, John 77, 85
Holden, Bowen 3, 92, 104
Hyland, Drew 35

Jackson, Casey 160
Jacques, Alfie................................ 21
Jamieson, Sid 5, 6, 7, 101, 173
Jenkins, Kathy 21
Jorgenson, Brad 54, 74, 145
Josephson, Michael 134

Kleinfelder, Carol 26
Kohn, Peter 80
Koudelka, Steve 103, 148
Kridel, Wendy ... 10, 13, 74, 76, 80, 99

Lasagna, Peter 12, 15, 16, 168
Leimsieder, Eric 48
Light, Jack 107
Long, Jeff 80, 96

Mangan, Terry 84
McCann,Emily 191, 192
McCoy, Alan 8, 50, 103, 77, 85
Millon, Erin Brown 27, 28, 29, 50
Murphy, Mike 123

Nasato, Brad 74, 80, 95, 99

Osherson, Sam 90, 105

Palumb, Matt 18
Paradis, Chris 9, 18, 74, 148,
155, 167, 191, 194, 195,
Pfeifer, Rob 45, 55, 113
Piatelli, Jack 125
Pietramala, Dave 18, 104, 148,
155, 167, 191

Piper, John 6, 90, 78
Pirani, John 3, 4, 18, 46, 48,
      53, 87, 94, 97, 119, 158, 159

Quinn, Erin 2, 5, 15, 19, 93
Quinn, Rob 18, 93, 73, 79, 81

Riitano, Jenny 185
Rotatori, Al 72, 80, 189
Ryan, Kevin 55, 134, 136

Sardella, John 159, 176
Schimoler, Paul 19, 20
Seaman, Tony 2, 22, 23
Shriver, Bob 168
Sieben, Paul 100
Simmons Jr., Roy 21, 24, 107, 108
Sopracasa, Eric 10, 37
Stahl, Sue 50
Stanton, Shaun 54, 78, 127
Starsia, Dom 22, 53, 63, 64,
      122, 187
Stephan, Dee 8, 43, 52, 96,
      104, 106, 144
Stevenson, Bob 92

Tierney, Bill 17, 157
Tighe, Jim 77, 110
Tigner, Steve 128
Timchal, Cindy 27, 28

Urick, Dave 2, 3, 17, 18, 145, 149

Van Arsdale, Marc 24, 183

Waldron, Jennifer 21
Waymack, Mark 34
Webb, Gordon 51, 104, 161
Werder, Adam 186
Wilcox, Mike 150
Williams, Jay 12, 16,
Wilson, Jim 51, 117, 127
Wolff, Alex 19

Zacoi, Tom 174
Zanella, Gene 11, 12, 93,
      100, 125, 184

References

Introduction

p. VI   Martin Seligman is a pioneer in the field of positive psychol-
        ogy and has authored, *Authentic Happiness*, London: Brealey.

Chapter 1

p. 1   The North American Indian Traveling College authored and
        published *Tewaarthon: Akwesasne's Story of Our National
        Game* in 1978.

p. 3   Neil Duffy's *The Spirit in the Stick* is a must read. It
        captures the essence of the culture and character of
        lacrosse.

p. 6   Rollo May's last book was *The Cry for Myth*. He pointed
        out that a big problem in the twentieth century was our
        loss of values.

p. 19   Lacrosse is the subject of the main feature article in the
        April 20, 2005 issue of *Sports Illustrated*, The article, "Get
        on the Stick," was written by *Sports Illustrated* senior
        writer Alexander Wolff and includes special reporting from
        Julia Morrill.

p. 21   For a more detailed perspective of sport specialization,
        refer to Jennifer Waldron (Michigan State University's Insti-
        tute for the Study of Youth Sports) *Stress, Overtraining,
        and Burnout Associated with Participation in Sport : Is
        Your Child at Risk*, http://ed-web3.educ.msu.edu/ysi/
        Spotlight2000/stress.htm

Chapter 2

p. 34   Mark H. Waymack (1996). Narrative *Ethics in the Clinical
        Setting*. In Making the Rounds in Health, Faith and Ethics.
        M. Marty (Ed.). Chicago: The Park Ridge Center.

p. 35   Drew Hyland, Opponents, Contestants, and Competitors:
        The Dialectic of Sport," *Journal of the Philosophy of Sport*,
        Vol. 11 (1985), pp. 63-70.

p. 37   Alice von Hildebrand *By Grief Defined, Letters to a Widow* (1994) Franciscan University Press.

p. 38   *A Farewell to Arms* is one of Ernest Hemingway's earliest novels.

p. 38   John Corlett's presentation is included in the "Proceedings of the Fourteenth Annual Conference on Counseling Athletes," Springfield College, May 1988.

p. 43   The *Pay it Forward Foundation* website is http://www.payitforwardfoundation.org/home.html

Chapter 3

p. 59   Kevin Ryan and James Cooper are the authors of *Those Who Can, Teach. (7ᵗʰ ed.)*. Boston: Houghton-Mifflin

p. 60   Steve Glenn and Joel Warner (1984) *Developing Capable Young People.* Hurst, Texas: Humansphere, Inc.

p. 64   James Kouzes and Barry Posner wrote *The Leadership Challenge* (2002) Jossey-Bass.

p. 83   Lee Smith – Trust March 1996 *Self*

Chapter 4

p. 90   Carol Hotchkiss spoke on these concepts as a keynote speaker at the Spring 1999 Independent School Health Association (ISHA) conference at Phillips Exeter Academy.

p. 96   M. Boyea, *Elements of Sport Leadership: A Comparison of High School Boy's Basketball Coaches with Varying Won-Loss Records,* unpublished doctoral dissertation, University of Maryland, 1994.

p. 105 Robert K. Greenleaf *Servant Leadership – A Journey into the Nature of Legitimate Power and Greatness* (1991) The Robert Greenleaf Center. The Paulist Press.

p. 105 Marian Wright Edelman is the founder and president of the Children's Defense Fund, has been an outspoken advocate for children's rights and for social support for children's well-being.

Chapter 5

p. 121 Jeff Beedy's _Sports Plus: Developing Youth Sports Programs that Teach Positive Values_ (Hamilton, MA: Project Adventure, 1997), pp. 61-89.

p. 130 Steve Tigner's version of "Aristotle's Six Moral States" is presented in the course, Cultural Foundations for Educators 1, at Boston University. The figure can be found in his course packet, _Outlines and Reading Aids for Aristotle's Nichomachean Ethics_ (1994).

p. 131 Ken Dryden authored the report, _Evaluation of Aigles Bleus' Hockey Program_ (Universite DeMoncton, June 1996).

p. 132 Sportsmanship and gamesmanship definitions from _The American Heritage ® Dictionary of the English Language, Fourth Edition_ Copyright © 2000 by Houghton Mifflin Company©

p. 132 Frank Deford _Gamesmanship vs. Sportsmanship Sports Illustrated – The Inside Game._ September 01, 1999. http://sportsillustrated.cnn.com/inside_game/deford/news/1999/09/01/deford/

p. 134 Michael Josephson The Josephson Institute. _Sportsmanship vs. Gamesmanship._ http://www.tothenextlevel.org/docs/coaches_corner/program_development/gamesmanship_vs_sportsmanship/default.asp

p. 134 Ryan, K. and Bohlin, K.E. _Building Character in Schools – Practical Ways to Bring Moral Instruction to Life._ San Francisco: Jossey-Bass, (1999). _Views values and virtues._

p. 137 Russell Gough, _Character Is Everything: Promoting Ethical Excellence in Sports_ (1997). Fort Worth, TX: Harcourt Brace.

Chapter 6

p. 143 E.J. Delattre – _Sport: A Crucible of Aspiration._ Presented at Character and Coaching conference at Boston University, Spring 1999.

p. 144 Keynote address by Dr. Peter Greer, Headmaster of The Montclair Kimberley Academy, at the "Reclaiming the Purpose of Sport" Conference. (Montclair, NJ, November, 1999)

p. 145 For a more comprehensive view of the flow model, see Csikszentmihalyi, M, *Flow: The Psychology of Optimal Experience* (New York: HarperCollins, 1990)

p. 150 *The Factors of Skilled Performance* figure was created by Leonard D. Zaichkowsky, Professor of Education at Boston University and Gerald A. Larson, former head of school, Cheshire Academy in *Physical, Motor and Fitness Development in Children and Adolescents.*

p. 152 For more information on performance excellence, see Yuri Hanin's *Emotions in Sport.*(Champaign, IL: Human Kinetics, 1999).

p. 153 The "Zones of Optimal Performance" illustration is an adaptation from Landers, D.M. and Boutcher, S.H. *Arousal Performance Relationships.* In Applied Sport Psychology – Personal Growth to Peak Performance. Jean Williams, Ed. (Mountain View, CA: Mayfield Publishing). p. 207.

p. 163 R. Kegan, *The Evolving Self* (Cambridge, MA: Harvard University Press, 1983).

p. 163 Bandura, A. Self-efficacy, *The Exercise of Control* (New York: WH Freeman, 1997) p. 391-392

p. 165 Gladwell, M. *The Physical Genius.* The New Yorker, August 2, 1999. p. 57-65.

p. 165 Adam Naylor's 2001 doctoral dissertation is entitled *The developmental environment of elite athletics: an evolving system*

p. 168 John Underwood is the founder of the American Athletic Institute. He has conducted significant research in the area of alcohol use on elite athletic performance.

p. 170 Dr. Alex Packer is the president of Boston-based FCD Educational Services. He is also the author of *Parenting One Day at a Time: Using the Tools of Recovery to Become Better Parents and Raise Better Kids.* (Center City, Minnesota: Hazeldon, 1996)

Chapter 7

p. 174 Tom Zacoi authored the *College Athletic Recruitement Handbook –A Guide for the Peters Township High School Girl's Lacrosse Team.*

p. 176 John Sardella wrote the manual *How to Start a Successful Lacrosse Program* in 2000 to help others set up a proper youth lacrosse program in their community.

p. 180 Shane Murphy, the author of *The Cheers and the Tears – A Healthy Alternative to the Dark Side of Youth Sports Today.* (1999) Jossey-Bass.

Endgame

p. 189 Alice Von Hildebrand is an internationally known lecturer, philosopher, and author. She cites Marcel in Grief Refined, Letters to a Widow (1994) Franciscan University Press.

p. 190 Robert Kegan, *The Evolving Self* (1983) Harvard University Press.

US Lacrosse

113 W. University Parkway
Baltimore, MD 21210-3300
410.235.6882 / 410.366.6735 (fax)
www.uslacrosse.org   info@uslacrosse.org

US LACROSSE IS HERE TO HELP!

Founded on January 1, 1998 as the national, non-profit governing body of men's and women's lacrosse, US Lacrosse unites the national lacrosse community around one organization to effectively serve the sport. The mission of US Lacrosse is to ensure a unified and responsive organization that develops and promotes the sport by providing services to its members and programs to inspire participation, while preserving the integrity of the game. In addition to our national headquarters, over fifty regional chapter organizations around the country help to fulfill this mission. Please visit www.uslacrosse.org or contact us for more information on how we can help you succeed as a lacrosse coach, official, player, administrator or fan.

All members of US Lacrosse have access to the following benefits:

- Affiliation with a local US Lacrosse Chapter

- *Lacrosse Magazine*, the sport's premier feature magazine and access to www.laxmagazine.com

- Receipt of the monthly US Lacrosse member E-mail Newsletter

- A comprehensive lacrosse insurance program for players, coaches, officials and events

- Developmental assistance for new teams and leagues; includes resources grants and New Start program

- Ongoing coordination of safety and injury research, including risk-management information

- Access to the US Lacrosse Sportsmanship Card Initiative

- The Lacrosse Museum &National Hall of Fame, the national archives of men's and women's lacrosse
- Member discounts on US Lacrosse merchandise and educational resources
- US Lacrosse is a national partner of the Positive Coaching Alliance

US Lacrosse proudly celebrates five years of collaboration with Positive Coaching Alliance (PCA), based out of the Stanford University Athletic Department (California). US Lacrosse and PCA have partnered in a nationwide endeavor to make lacrosse a positive, character-building experience for every athlete and to make the experience a more successful one for coaches, parents, fans and officials. For more information about PCA please visit www.uslacrosse.org or www.positivecoach.org

US LACROSSE RESOURCES

Additional information regarding all resources offered through US Lacrosse can be found on the US Lacrosse website at www.uslacrosse.org.

US Lacrosse Resources for Coaches

- Game leadership and development through the Men's and Women's Division Coaches Councils
- Online learning opportunities through the Coaches Education On-line Courses
- On-field and classroom learning opportunities through the Coaches Education Instructional Clinics
- Premier educational opportunity to attend the annual US Lacrosse National Convention; includes classroom clinic sessions and live field demonstrations
- Access to the US Lacrosse Risk Management Manual
- Ability to purchase Coach's educational and instructional rule books, manuals, videos and DVDs

US Lacrosse Resources for Officials and Umpires

- Game leadership and development through the Men's and Women's Division Officials Councils
- On-field and classroom learning opportunities through the Men's and Women's Officials Training Sessions
- Premier educational opportunity to attend the annual US Lacrosse National Convention; includes classroom clinics, rules interpretations and live field demonstrations
- Ability to purchase Official's educational and instructional rule books, manuals, videos and DVDs

US Lacrosse Resources for Players

- Game leadership and development through the Men's and Women's Division Athletes Council
- On-field educational opportunity through regional US Men's and Women's National Team clinics
- Participation in special events such as the US Lacrosse National Youth Festivals, Women's Division National Tournament and Intercollegiate Associates National Championships, and numerous tournaments around the country
- Access to the US Lacrosse Pursuing College Play program
- Ability to purchase Player's educational and instructional manuals, videos and DVDs

US Lacrosse Resources for Administrators

- On-line web data access for managing your program
- Access to the US Lacrosse Best Practices
- Ability to obtain event/clinic/tournament insurance coverage through US Lacrosse insurance partner
- Access to the League Administration Sexual Harassment Manual and Policy